I S

David Rebbettes and David Oliver

ISBN 978-0-9574352-0-9

Printed in the UK

Second Edition

Introduction

This book is a collection of real-life stories from business owners who have sold their businesses in the past few years. As an author with the responsibility and privilege of interviewing each of the business owners, I have made a number of striking and unexpected discoveries.

The first surprise was the number of people who were more than willing to be interviewed. I have sold a business myself and I can't remember ever talking to anyone about my story, so why was it that these business owners were so keen?

The second surprise was the amazing variety of reasons given for the decision to sell. For example, one story movingly describes Callum, a seven-year-old boy with a tear-stained face, holding his dad's hand, desperately trying to stop him going to work again on a Saturday...

A common motive for the majority of those interviewed was concern for the welfare of the business itself, and in particular the future welfare of the staff employed in the business. In the cases described in this book's 11 chapters, all the staff who wanted to stay with the business have done so, and the proportion of staff who chose to is close to 100%.

The biggest surprise of all was that no-one we interviewed really celebrated their sale. You and I could be excused for thinking that selling a business for a great price would be a cause of great celebration, but we'd be wrong. When we questioned the contributors to find out why this phenomenon was so marked, the reason we were most frequently given was that at the point of sale there was a real sense of loss. One owner described this moment as like 'losing a child that I had brought to birth,' and for some it took a few months to adjust after the sale.

But don't worry! It's equally true that for every person

interviewed, and in every case featured in this book, the final outcome has been satisfying, deeply satisfying, for the exiting owner or shareholder.

Health has been restored, dreams have been fulfilled, and stress and strain have become a distant memory. New horizons of positive choice have opened up for every man and woman, and no-one has regretted the deal...

Enjoy these stories!

David Oliver, Author.

Contents

THE FINISHING TOUCH

Like most of us, Mel Atkins can remember the day he started his business. In his case, it was April Fools' Day 1989. As he says, 'If it all went wrong, at least we could tell the bank it was just a big joke!' Previously working with a leisure company specialising in riverboat cruises, Mel had become fed up with the attitude and culture of his employer. Suppliers were paid late, quality and value for the client were poor, and as the Operations Director he spent much of his life fending off complaints.

From time to time Mel would complain to his friends, and they would typically respond by suggesting he should man it up, stop complaining and start his own business. So it was, in a two-bedroom flat in Tooting Bec at the age of 29, that Mel launched The Finishing Touch. Starting with the complaints file from his previous job, he searched for new clients. His prestigious office was the corner of his living room, where he had a badly assembled MFI desk and a well-worn second-hand filing cabinet; stacks of papers covered the dining room table.

Mel was pitching for high-value work and wanted his business to appear big enough, so he invented two fictitious members of staff – Dale Roberts, an Australian who was his sales manager, and Mike Stevens, head of advertising.

Any sales reps calling in would be directed to the non-existent Mike Stevens, who never seemed to return calls. Any mailshots or promotional brochures sent out carried the name Dale Roberts. In this way, if a caller asked for Mike Stevens, Mel would know immediately it was a sales rep hustling for business and they would get short shrift. If a caller asked for Dale Roberts, Mel could be sure that here was a potential client, and the sales process would kick in.

'Every day was fun, and the team spirit and camaraderie were at an all-time high.'

Within three months, Mel's wife Julie joined him, working with the team's first cell phone, which had a battery life of just one hour!

The Finishing Touch's next office was located in Mel and Julie's second home. An old coach house in their Richmond property was converted to take four desks, with a small area designated for filing. Mel looks back wistfully on those days: 'They were some of our best times. Every day was fun, and the team spirit and camaraderie were at an all-time high.'

Even the negative elements of the environment were somehow full of fun. From time to time, spiders would drop onto staff from the exposed rafters. One key member of staff who had a real fear of spiders had to work all day with a hat on! The age and condition of the heating in the property meant staff would frequently sit there cold, wearing several jumpers. A golden retriever puppy was added to the mix and would often sit in and join the fun. In fact, if you happened to be an onlooker, on some days it would be quite possible to see a staff member wearing a hat, with a dog on her lap, busily discussing a large project involving 800 people and a budget of £200k. Those days were fun.

The first doubts

A move to a new office environment in 1999 saw the company's turnover reach nearly £5 million. But an unexpected change began to nibble away at Mel's sense of entrepreneurial enjoyment.

As the staff moved out of the home-based environment and into a more formal office setting, attitudes changed. New furniture, an attractive boardroom and a staff dining area with a new microwave seemed to trigger a new employee attitude. Instead of the relaxed team spirit of earlier years, staff now became more obsessed with health care, employer's liability, pay rises and office rules. Now instead of being friends, Mel and Julie became the bosses, and the individuals in the team became the employees. Staff would arrange a drinks evening, and Mel and Julie would no longer be invited.

This unexpected and unwelcome change began to sow the seeds of doubt for Mel. It's a common reason for clients to turn to BCMS Corporate, and it's often referred to as the 'entrepreneur versus manager' condition. It's quite common for a business to get to a certain size and for the founder or owner to no longer enjoy the experience. Human resources, staff challenges, red tape and the daily management of seemingly trivial issues can wear down even the most optimistic person. And so it was for Mel. What was once a 'band of brothers' became an office full of employees – and that change took its toll.

Two tragedies

Two tragedies were to significantly shape the growth of the business and indirectly shape Mel's own future. In August 1989 the Marchioness pleasure boat sank on the River Thames with the loss of 51 lives. The subsequent wholesale withdrawal of corporate events from the Thames spurred Mel to seek out a different style of corporate event, land-based, with high-quality venues and high-quality experiences.

What was once a 'band of brothers', became an office full of employees – and that change took its toll.

Following this change of direction, the business began to grow steadily. In the first year, The Finishing Touch organised a Christmas party for Andersen Consulting (soon to become Accenture) for 120 people. The quality of service provided that night (including having a representative on site for the whole event) led to an invitation to visit their offices and pitch to a number of departments. That small, high-quality Christmas party led to commissions to manage regular summer balls for Accenture, typically involving up to 2,000 people. These major

events would dramatically increase the credibility and perceived competence of the Finishing Touch team, growing its range of services and giving it an enviable client list.

The second tragedy was also destined to change The Finishing Touch, and with it Mel's future. The business sailed through the difficulties and challenges of the new millennium, but the devastating impact of the 9/11 attack on New York's twin towers in 2001 led to an industry-wide cutback in corporate events, and the simultaneous recession saw The Finishing Touch lose half of its business.

In the middle of this period, Accenture tightened its procurement process, and in so doing it reduced the amount spent on each event. For Mel this meant significant reductions in profit.

These were lean times for the industry, and lean times indeed for Mel. While hunting for work in this tough period, The Finishing Touch was offered 35 training days in the public sector. The work was low-margin and hard graft, and Mel was reluctant, but recessionary pressures prevailed. With the job completed and the client delighted, the opportunity came to tender for a three-year contract. Mel was resistant. From his experience of the previous 35 days he knew this contract would inevitably take its toll on him, on the family and on the business, and so he stalled.

Unsurprisingly, he came under pressure to complete the tender document. He responded reluctantly and half-heartedly. To his horror, The Finishing Touch was awarded the tender, with 100 training days requested in the following three months.

While all these events were taking place, things were changing in the Atkins family. At around this time, Mel and Julie's first child Callum was born. Coupled with the business changes they were experiencing, this too was to have a profound impact on Mel and his future choices.

Help! We want our lives back!

As Mel and Julie had dreaded, for the next few years the workload increased inexorably. Mel found himself working all day Saturday and part of every Sunday, catching up with admin and invoicing for hundreds of events. More staff were employed, and 80 to 90 hour weeks became the norm.

A crunch moment came in 2004. Even in these busy, life-sapping times Mel managed to squeeze out a tiny bit of time to take Callum to football practice on Saturday mornings. Returning from this early one Saturday with his little hand tucked happily inside his dad's, Callum turned and said to Mel, 'Dad, coach says I have to practise, so can we play football today, please?' Mel remembers the dilemma in his mind and his pain as Callum, sensing his hesitation, looked up with a tear-stained face and said, 'You're going to work, aren't you?'

Callum went indoors angry and tearful, desperately upset. Mel was left reflecting on the sobering truth: as he put it, 'I can't even give my son 10 minutes of my time when he needs it.'

*'I can't even give my son 10 minutes of
my time when he needs it.'*

To make matters worse, Julie was feeling the strain too. With Mel working from 7am to 7.30pm, she was telling him 'You can't keep doing this' – yet all the while understanding that for the business to survive, he and they had no choice. It felt like a nightmare from which they would never wake. They both felt guilty and they both felt trapped.

The challenges from Julie and the heart-breaking exchange with Callum left an indelible mark on Mel. He turned to Julie that evening and said, 'Julie, this isn't working. We're going to have to sell the business.'

He did not speak the thought nagging inside him – that this was easier said than done.

Selling up
Mel's first port of call was his firm of accountants. He found this experience utterly frustrating and disappointing. They simply did not have the knowledge or competence to help.

The next step was to approach some corporate finance advisers – three in total. In each case they were only interested in the historic accounts. The response from each one was the same: 'You need three more good years, then come back in and talk.'

Feeling discouraged and somewhat disillusioned, Mel responded to a mailshot from the BCMS Corporate office in Kingsclere. His recollection of the first meeting was that this was very different.

Mel came out of his first meeting with BCMS's Business Development Director Malcolm saying, 'The session was like therapy – it was so encouraging. Malcolm asked me questions like, "Why do you want to sell, what do you want to achieve?" – questions no-one else had asked, questions that got me thinking positively and got me in the right frame of mind.'

Mel remembers saying to Malcolm, 'Do you want to see my accounts?' Malcolm's reply was 'Not at this stage!' The process left Mel and Julie with hope.

Malcolm's positive and encouraging questioning style also helped Mel and Julie to think through the ideal outcome from their potential sale. This was something they hadn't even considered before. And the outcomes the two desired were both different and both achievable. While Julie wanted to exit the business, Mel really wanted to stay working in it, doing what he enjoyed most – growing the business and meeting clients – with someone else taking responsibility for the systems, the staff and the paperwork.

Can I do this?

The difference in BCMS's approach to selling a business was both clear and positive. But now Mel had to wrestle with his own thoughts and the personal challenge that the big decision represented. For 18 years this business had been his. He had grown it from nothing in the two-bedroom flat in Tooting Bec to an attractive £5 million business today. This was his baby, and he was emotional at the thought of losing it.

Plus there were the staff. Even with the changes over the years, these people had been loyal, hard-working contributors to the success he and Julie had enjoyed. They were great people, and he felt responsible. The future of the staff lay in the outcome of this decision.

Mel recalls the moment etched in his mind when he pressed the button on his fax machine to send the formal order confirmation through to BCMS Corporate. 'I was so torn by making the final decision that as the paper went through the machine I grabbed at the end of it, trying to stop it.' Nevertheless, the fax went through.

The long journey

The fax had been sent in less than 60 seconds, but the sale process would last for nearly 12 months. For Mel the process was quite stressful at times, and having Mark, the BCMS deal leader, alongside made a huge difference. Mark prepared Mel for possible outcomes; he walked him through every negotiation scenario they could conceivably face.

Continuing to run the business during this time was tough, especially since he had to keep the process confidential. There were days when Mel felt he had lost the will to live. At those times Mark would keep him on track. Mel's recollection was that Mark never once lost faith or confidence that The Finishing Touch would eventually sell.

The BCMS process identified 285 potential acquirers, with 85 of these entering initial discussion and 13 getting into serious negotiative dialogue. The final bidding stage came down to five companies.

Mel recalls having doubts at every one of the 13 meetings organised by BCMS. One particular challenge was that the potential acquirer's first question would invariably be about Mel's own future in the business. 'Mel,' they would say, 'in essence you are the business: how can we be sure you'll stay and that you'll also remain motivated?' Mel says that at these times having the BCMS negotiator there to handle the questions with him was an absolute lifesaver.

Handling the bids was another area where the support from BCMS was critical. When the first bid came through, Mel was delighted and suggested to the BCMS team that they accept it. Carefully but insistently the BCMS team explained how unsatisfactory the bid was, especially as it was based primarily on a paper transaction, i.e. shares. The bid was summarily despatched.

Mel was also still concerned about his staff and their future. He made sure that the BCMS team knew this was a very important ingredient in the mix. Equally, he was certain that the business could not survive and carry on as it was. A deal simply had to be done, and it had to be the right one.

In September 2005 the negotiation team at BCMS secured the right deal – good for Mel and Julie, good for the staff and very good for the future of the business.

Where were you?
When a business sale is finally concluded, the memory is different for every shareholder, but whatever the memories, they are always etched into the mind. Mel remembers the day his deal was finally done and the money transferred. It was 13 September 2005, his mum's birthday. England's cricket team had beaten Australia to win the Ashes, and at Mel's hotel (the City Grange) the manager had given a cigar to Freddie Flintoff, voted Player of the Series, and seen Freddie eat it rather than smoke it. Walking from this bizarre incident at the City Grange to the lawyers – Clintons – for the final transaction, Mel passed through Trafalgar Square as the England team bus came by. Mel found himself singing 'Jerusalem', dressed in his best suit and carrying his briefcase. His was the only suit and briefcase visible in news footage shown later featuring the tens of thousands of England supporters.

The final moments of the transaction were almost an anticlimax for Mel. He shared some champagne with Julie before heading off to an event that The Finishing Touch was running that day. After the event Mel took time individually with each member of staff to tell them about the sale, explaining to each of them how their new future would look and how they could benefit in terms of growth and career progression. When that was done, he had a sense of positive relief, an overwhelming conviction that they had made the right choice and achieved the right outcome.

Happily ever after?

Mel has enjoyed the last few years, helping the business to grow to £8 million with profits of £1.8 million. But more importantly, he has his life back, Julie has a husband back and Callum has his dad back.

Mel and Julie have been able to rebuild their house and achieve many things that before the sale there was no time for. At the time of the sale, Mel and Julie were planning to travel the world; instead they now have three-year-old twins, George and Harry!

The first thing Mel did was to take a cricket coaching badge and begin coaching Callum's cricket team, which he still does today. He also started a football team with Callum and a few friends for under-11s. That has gone so well that they now have two full teams and a waiting list.

If Callum's earlier tear-filled exchange was a trigger for selling the business, today his appreciation of the way his dad coaches him and his friends is proof of the pudding. It's appropriate to leave the last words of this chapter to Callum: 'Dad, you're a really good coach, and my friends think so too.'

Fact file

The business

The Finishing Touch is a full-service events management business. It was grown from a husband-and-wife start-up in a two-bedroom flat in 1989 to a £5 million turnover business at the point of sale.

The reason for sale

The main reason for the sale was the urgent need to find a change in lifestyle. Mel Atkins was routinely working 90-hour weeks, and he and his wife Julie wanted their lives back. Mel also found the day-to-day management a grind. As an entrepreneur, he enjoyed the business development, but the staff challenges, red tape and the daily administrative grind were wearing him down. Julie wanted to leave the business altogether; Mel wanted to stay on and enjoy the business development role without the headache of administrative management responsibility.

The outcome

BCMS Corporate identified 285 potential acquirers. Eighty-seven requested further information and 13 of those entered negotiative dialogue.

Five firm offers were received, and the final sale price agreed was £3.53 million. The successful offer was not selected on the basis of the highest price: it was chosen because it was the best deal for Mel and Julie, their staff and the ongoing future of the business.

NETWORK EUROPE GROUP

Snow adds to the drama

Dean Rayment and the Network Europe Group Limited (NEG) team remember 30 November 2010 very well. This was a day they had been anticipating, planning for and motivated towards. It was the day when the sale of NEG was due to be concluded. But it was also the day when snow brought roads, airports and train services in the UK to a standstill. The NEG shareholders weren't even able to drive to the station for the journey to London, essential for the final legal stages of the sale. This was unexpected and unwelcome last-minute drama: more about its resolution shortly!

NEG specialises in providing fixed-line telephone solutions to the primary health care sector in the UK through its pioneering Surgery LineTM offering. The Surgery Line telephony solution typically comprises network services (including inbound calls and line rental), telephony hardware, installation and support, software and maintenance contracts. Dean Rayment, the outgoing MD, tells the story on behalf of the shareholders:

At the time of exit, NEG's turnover was £12.6 million, with earnings before interest and taxes (EBIT) of £3.7 million and nine shareholders. Ordinarily that fact alone would bring huge complications and added stress to a potential sale, but in this case the process was remarkably stress-free, with a great outcome. With insights from the team helping us to prepare for any sale with multiple shareholders, we achieved a final sale price of £23.86 million.

A beginning with the end in sight

Dean Rayment's own journey had humble beginnings. After a first role in sales, he worked his way through the ranks, becoming Sales Manager and then Associate Customer Accounts Director. In 2003 Dean and three other managers decided on a management buyout (MBO), which was successfully completed in 2004.

From the very beginning, the stated aim of the shareholders was to grow the business from its £2.3 million ceiling into a substantial and profitable small to medium enterprise (SME), with a trade sale as a five-year target. The importance of this clear and stated aim – disposal in five years – was to pay dividends when the time came for the sale process.

The team put it this way: 'All nine of us are entrepreneurs, and we know the reality is that nothing lasts for ever, so our thought process was: how long can we continue to grow this business? How big can we grow it? How can we get the best possible outcome?'

> *This clear and stated aim – disposal in five years – was to pay dividends.*

Dean's unequivocal view is that any company that hasn't got an exit strategy hasn't got it right. The shareholders had A, B and C options for exit in the bottom drawer. From the very beginning it was their intention to get to a position where they could have an exit strategy with a variety of options. None of them wanted to end up with only one option. That was their thinking, and that is how they planned.

Innovation and growth

The first big gamble for the new team was developing the Surgery Line concept. At the time, it was an innovative and untested concept, a solution to enhance telephony for the National Health Service (NHS), specifically for general practitioners (GPs) and dentists. Each month 20 million patients were attempting to contact their GP by phone. Around half of these callers were met with the brick wall of an engaged tone, denying them access by telephone to local health care. The Surgery Line solution changed all that, enabling GPs and other primary care professionals to improve patient access and reduce complaints. The patients got a dramatically improved experience.

This ground-breaking service, and the measurable benefit it brought to health care providers, helped the NEG team ride out the largely unexpected recession. The company continued to grow even during that recession because Surgery Line was tightly defined in a vertical niche: GPs within the NHS. At the time this niche market remained largely untouched by recessionary pressures, bills got paid, and with government targets putting pressure on GPs it was little wonder that more than 16% of surgeries took on the Surgery Line solution. NEG experienced good growth.

During the ensuing five-year period, various parts of the group were consolidated and the business grew from its modest MBO starting point of £2.3 million turnover to a 2010 figure of £12.6 million. For each of the three years prior to consolidation, the billing arm of NEG won a place in the Sunday Times Tech Track 100 league table. (The Tech Track table ranks Britain's 100 fastest-growing private tech companies.) NEG was also ranked in the Tech Track 'Top 10' in 2007 and 2008, and made the Top 100 list again in 2009.

The awards consolidated NEG's position as the company with the most successful telephony solution for the NHS market. As one of the shareholders said, 'This might well be the best time to look at selling the business.'

Quicker than we thought

Thinking more seriously about the positive implications of the timing, Dean and three other shareholders proposed to the board that the exit process begin with immediate effect. To their surprise there was unanimity. The board tasked Dean and his colleagues Craig Hughes and Scott Russell to act as the exit team and to find a supporting agent or consultant who could help ensure there would be multiple options on the table.

The options they considered included selling all or part of the business, investor purchase, trade sale or private sale. Most important to all nine shareholders was the well-being of their staff. Many key staff had been with the business for 10 years or more, and the shareholders wanted to ensure that any deal provided the best possible future for them.

Dean and his exit team colleagues began the process of short-listing potential mergers and acquisitions (M&A) specialists. They vetted three – one large, one small and one mid-size corporate finance company – before deciding to engage BCMS Corporate.

BCMS was selected for a number of reasons, including a recommendation from Coutts Bank. For the exit team, the choice was straightforward: 'The BCMS process seemed the most likely to give us the best possible outcome for our own aspirations, and also the best possible outcome for our staff. The wide range of disposals experience, and the overseas competence BCMS offered, left us feeling comfortable that we had the best possible chance of the best possible outcome.'

The intensity and speed of the process surprised the team a little. From that boardroom agreement in January 2010, BCMS was appointed in February, and on 1 December the sale was completed.

Essential agreement

Nine shareholders in a disposal is not a record, but it is reasonably challenging! For nine shareholders to come to agreement about the decision to sell in the first place, to select the right buyer, and finally to agree terms to suit all nine, is no mean feat.

Ever since the early days of the MBO, the shareholders had worked hard to ensure that they all had clear expectations and aspirations. When it came to executing the exit plan, six of the shareholders wanted to exit, while three ideally wanted to stay on and work with the new owners. All nine shareholders were unanimous in wanting the best deal for the staff too.

> *All nine shareholders were unanimous in wanting the best deal for the staff.*

Every potential buyer was made aware that six of the shareholders would leave the deal table and walk away, and three would be staying. The position was made clear in each conversation: these three shareholders are the workforce foundation, the key staff, and whoever finally acquires NEG gets them.

Stepping back

Another challenge facing Dean and his fellow director Scott in the exit team was their entrepreneurial spirit. Both had always assumed that they would personally drive the final exit process. As far as they were concerned, no-one knew the business as well as they did, and no-one could possibly know the industry better than they did. Plus they were both experienced and successful negotiators. Both of them had been in the business since the early 1990s. They had been involved in all kinds of negotiations, including large and small contracts, MBOs, management buy-ins and exit strategies.

However, they very quickly realised that they had to take one step

back, for the good of the final outcome. It became obvious that any buyer would probably offer as little as they thought they could get away with, and in the process would say things that emotionally Dean and Scott were likely to react to. For both of them this was a tough decision. As Dean put it, 'Over years, we had taken the business through the tough times and through the good times. I knew we were inclined to get emotional about our "baby", and very early on we had to make the decision to somehow rein in our emotions, stay professional and stay composed.'

For the exit team, that meant allowing the BCMS negotiator to take responsibility and to control the negotiation process. Dean expressed the strong conviction of the team: 'I would absolutely recommend to anyone selling a business that you bring someone like BCMS to the negotiation table, because the experience they've gained from negotiating one UK company sale every four days means you'll get a high standard of professional competence, emotion is taken out of the transaction, and you're far more likely to get the best possible valuation.'

The process

BCMS identified more than 130 potential acquirers. The exit team whittled that down to the 110 most likely contenders, which in turn resulted in 20 Non-Disclosure Agreements (NDAs) and Information Memorandums (IMs). Subsequently eight serious negotiation dialogues took place, with two in the penultimate round and the successful bidder winning exclusivity in the final round.

As Dean recalls, there were no really tense moments. The board had already commissioned the exit team to work with Andrew, the BCMS Deal Leader. In reality, because of the large number of meetings involved, it was agreed early on that Dean would take the main role in presenting the company. He would draw in two of the three shareholders who were going to stay with the business, to answer any questions. Andrew would then lead the subsequent negotiations.

From the beginning, one concern for all the shareholders was their desire to safeguard the brand, especially Surgery Line. So much history was invested in the brand, so much emotional capital, that the team was determined to protect it. All nine were adamant that any successful deal should protect the staff and the office base from which the business was run. BCMS was alerted early on to the fact that asset stripping or staff loss would be an unacceptable outcome.

By being very clear about their aspirations from the outset, the exiting owners have achieved them all.

When it came to the final choice, the deciding factor was not just the 'cash sum'. The deal was good, but what the team liked was that the other terms were best for the exiting shareholders, the remaining shareholders and, more importantly, the entire staff. It was also best for the future of NEG itself. All the staff have kept their jobs, the business is continuing from the same offices, and the brand identity has been retained. By being very clear about their aspirations from the outset, the exiting owners have achieved them all.

It's done – and not a suit in sight!

You will probably recall the drama at the beginning of the chapter. The last days and hours of every deal can be intense, but this one was to be more intense than most – even the weather conspired to work against its completion. The deal was due to be finalised on 30 November, the day when the snow fell.

Dean's home is four miles from the nearest railway station. Leaving early, he had to give up halfway there, drive back home, then walk the four miles back to the station in ski clothing. He recalls all the other shareholders arriving at the solicitor's London office with similar stories, and all dressed in ski clothing and boots. Not one suit in sight!

The snow wasn't the only problem: the lawyers had last-minute questions, and some legal hitches arose, as a result of which completion did not happen on the day. The winter-clad gang of nine made their way home deflated and empty-handed – for that day at least.

The continuing transport difficulties caused by the snow made it necessary the next day to give the lawyer power of attorney. Each shareholder worked from home till 11 o'clock that night. When it was all done, they felt an overwhelming sense of relief. The congratulatory texts they sent each other were brief and to the point – 'It's done!'

Happy now?

For Dean, the process was emotional. He'd been involved in the business for more than 16 years, and now his baby was gone. Today, his memories of his time in the industry generally, and with NEG in particular, are rich and happy. He remembers his colleagues and customers with gratitude and great affection: 'They were a great bunch of people to work with.'

Waking up the following morning, Dean had two overarching emotions. His first thought was one of relief: 'I haven't got to take responsibility for anything, and I haven't got to turn up anywhere.' His second? 'This is the first time I've woken up unemployed.'

That changed pretty quickly. Two in five BCMS clients start a new business within 18 months. Dean has started two! He is still very much the entrepreneur, but now he is doing things at his own pace. Dean has always endeavoured to keep family and business separate, but in recent years, as he puts it, 'The family have suffered a bit.'

Things are very different now. His two children are over the moon and love having more time with Daddy. These days he makes it home for the children's dinner time most nights, and most mornings he makes breakfast for the family, enjoying the opportunity to share quality time with them. For Dean, family priorities are back in their proper place.

Dean's final words sum it all up: 'Before, it was work with a bit of life. Now it's life with a bit of work. I like that, and so does my family!'

Fact file

The business

NEG is the UK's leading provider of telephony solutions to the primary care sector. At the heart of the company's offering is Surgery LineTM, a revolutionary co-funded telephony solution supplied to GP and dental surgeries across the UK.

From a turnover of £2.3 million at the time of their MBO in 2004, the exiting shareholders in 2010 had grown the business to £12.6 million.

The reason for sale

At the start of the MBO process the plan was clear: the stated aim of the shareholders was to grow the business into a substantial and profitable SME, with a trade sale as the five-year target. The plan was to ensure that when the time came to sell, they would have a number of options.

The outcome

BCMS Corporate identified more than 130 potential acquirers. 20 signed an NDA and received an IM, and eight entered the negotiating process. The final offer accepted was £23.86 million.

Three shareholders wanted to remain with the company and did. Six shareholders wanted to walk away post-sale and did. The office, the staff and the brand were all protected in the terms of the deal. For shareholders, for staff and for the business itself, it was a good deal.

The new future

In common with other BCMS clients, Dean Rayment has subsequently started two new businesses, 67 Investment Ltd and Argyll Properties Ltd (APL), that together offer the following services:

Property portfolio: Buying multiple properties, freehold or leasehold on long-term options, with a view to providing a managed rental service to both residential and commercial. Plus acquiring land/properties for rebuild and development.

Consultancy: Providing help and advice to small to medium businesses.

Investment: Looking at opportunities that require an investment to allow them to grow, complete or expand.

To contact Dean, email: deanrayment10@gmail.com

MILSOM INDUSTRIAL DESIGNS

A different kind of start

Peter Kenny had run a business in engineering for many years, offering design and recruitment of technical staff. Looking for a new challenge, Peter sold his shares to his business partner and joined the board of Milsom in 2003. At that time Milsom was turning over just £1.4 million and was recovering from some recessionary difficulties. The company specialises in design, primarily in aerospace and defence. Project-based design is normally an upfront cost and often the first expenditure to be slashed in a recession, and that proved to be the case for Milsom.

Peter had known the other Milsom directors for 20 years, and at the back of his mind his reason for joining them was to support his friend Richard Moore. It was clear to both of them that they had very different and complementary skill sets. Richard was and is an outstanding salesman, capable of seeing opportunities and solutions that others miss. But that same unique hunter's skill inevitably meant that he was not so commercially oriented. Peter, on the other hand, did not share Richard's insightful business development instinct, but having built his own business from scratch and operated it for seven years, he had learned a lot about running a business. Peter's management capabilities and commercial instinct were pretty strong. He worked for three months as an employee, then bought 50% of the shares in the business from Richard and Carol Moore.

Early joys

Peter's previous company had a small in-house team, mostly site-based, and he was looking forward to running a much larger office. He had missed working with people and the fulfilment of being part of a larger team. When he joined it, Milson had 25 staff in-house. Peter found his workplace joie de vivre returning – he loved dealing with staff again and bringing his experience to bear in a variety of fulfilling ways.

Peter put it like this: 'The new business opportunities being identified were wonderful, and I could play to my strengths with cost control and project management. Richard was outstandingly good at finding new opportunities for work, in fact he couldn't stop himself, and the combination of those skills is what the business needed.'

At the same time, the business was being offered certain kinds of job that were not cost-effective to take on. Some clients and projects were in reality a risk to the business rather than a benefit. A number of contracts that had been taken on earlier were running at a loss. The new dynamic that their complementary skills brought would allow substantial business development, and in a more controlled, selective and profitable way. The business began to grow, and profits rose.

First thoughts

Peter and Richard started to think about selling the business in December 2008, when an approach was made out of the blue. That initial interest faded away, but soon afterwards they found themselves speaking to an international company that was also potentially interested. However, this opportunity too seemed to grind slowly to a halt.

With this 'erratic' experience, Peter and Richard decided to attend a BCMS seminar. Peter recalls: 'The logic was simple. We hadn't been this way before; we wanted to know how to assess what the business might be worth and who might buy it. In essence we wanted to listen to someone who sold businesses.'

Following the seminar, Peter and Richard went to a business evaluation meeting and found themselves being professionally challenged by the BCMS consultant. It was an interesting experience for them both, because the consultation focused on the fact that 88% of Milsom turnover was currently with one customer in the defence industry. An important question had to be answered: 'What would the true business value be if you were no longer the lead supplier to that customer?' A robust answer was required if the business was to sell for maximum value.

Milsom transformed

With the strong personal combination of the two directors, Milsom's turnover had grown to just under £7 million. The management structure had been developed significantly, with highly qualified and well trained managers and section leaders. A new accounts system had been developed. Proficient HR and recruitment systems and EU compliance had been put in place.

One of the company's primary areas of uniqueness – technical publications – was maturing measurably, with highly skilled employees, and the business was steadily reducing its dependence on the key players.

As directors, Peter and Richard found that their jobs had become easier. Peter reflected: 'We had become financially sound and profitable, and it began to make us play safe: in fact we would evaluate any sizeable new business opportunities almost solely in terms of risk. We were much less willing to grow another substantial part of the business – we were restricting the growth ourselves.'

Playing it safe

BCMS's experience would suggest that this is not uncommon in a growing business: owners get to a threshold where the investment, commitment or risk required to move the business on becomes too great. When directors or shareholders get to this stage, the business suffers from their inevitable tendency to play it safe and avoid risk.

Peter and Richard were crystal clear: the future growth and development of the business would require someone less risk-averse at the helm. Milsom needed a new owner who could take advantage of the potential to cross-trade and leverage the client base and the company's unique technical skills.

The future growth and development of the business would require someone less risk-averse at the helm.

Vetting the new owners

Peter and Richard determined that any purchaser would need to have an appropriate cultural understanding of their business. There were several pragmatic reasons for this stance. In view of the nature of the business, they assumed a purchaser would be very likely to want an earn-out period. For that to work effectively, both Peter and Richard had to feel comfortable with any acquirer's management style. The bigger challenge was with Milsom's major client: its approval would be critical. The client was very dependent on the 'Milsom way', which included response times and business relationship culture. Any deal that could potentially unsettle that relationship would be a non-starter.

For Peter and Richard this was to be straightforward. When they met interested parties with the BCMS team, they would observe the approach and attitude of the potential acquirers. The way these handled their approach, especially with regard to the more emotional parts of the negotiation dialogue, would give Peter and Richard a feel for the way they were likely to handle Milsom's major client. It would also reflect how they would conduct price negotiations with that client, and importantly how they would deal with Milsom's own staff. In one case, that led to a decision to withdraw from the negotiations at an early stage.

Aspirations made simple

Peter was clear in his aspirations. At the age of 58, he wanted the price achieved to reflect possible income for at least the following 10 years. Perhaps more importantly, those 10 years of income would also help build the future of his two older children. Without a job, he wanted to be sure he could see them established.

Equally, neither Peter nor Richard wanted to undersell what they

had worked so hard to establish. An important factor in the negotiating position was that both Peter and Richard were confident about their own future, even if the business didn't sell. The two directors had begun to delegate, and were both already down to a four-day week. They didn't have to sell the business at any cost.

Emotional roller-coaster

Peter's subsequent reflection on the negotiation process stirred some vivid memories. He commented on the range of attitudes that potential acquirers displayed. Some people looked seriously at the business, and even if ultimately it didn't suit them or their strategic aims, they were very complimentary and wished both directors well. Others were suspicious about the owners' intentions in leaving the business and made that plain. For both directors, that was emotionally upsetting.

Peter said: 'When you have a good business and it's profitable, you assume others will understand its value, but it's not that easy. If you've grown a profitable business with all the hard work done, you think it's all benefits, but they think it's all risk. Our first surprise was that they weren't queuing up with great offers.'

For Peter and Richard it was as though they had laid the golden egg, but the acquirer was wondering if they might be getting a poisoned chalice!

It was as though they had laid the golden egg, but the acquirer was wondering if they might be getting a poisoned chalice!

There were companies in a similar line of activity that couldn't understand why Milsom had such a good business at such significant levels with just one client. That would lead to suspicion that was very difficult to address.

Both Peter and Richard found it easier to deal with corporate entities rather than with individuals who had grown their own businesses. Individual responses were more likely to be emotional, rather than objective or financial. Some of the comments and questions arising from the IM were strange too, and left Peter and Richard with questions of their own. They found it especially difficult to understand why some firms were interested and others were not.

More surprises

Both directors found it quite shocking when potential acquirers came back and offered less than the value on the balance sheet, when the balance sheet made it clear what the business was worth. Other potential buyers who were engaged in the negotiation process restructured their offer four or five times so that in theory it looked better on paper – but when it was checked, there was no difference in substance. That was tiring.

Some acquirers appeared to be playing a negotiation game of 'How cheaply can we buy this?' They were not interested in buying at a proper price and certainly not interested in developing the business. Having the BCMS negotiator alongside at these times was helpful, both in terms of handling the emotional tension and also, more importantly, in making the right decisions with the right acquirers.

They experienced another jolt to the system when a firm potential acquirer offered a good deal but then unexpectedly pulled out because of a change of strategic instructions from HQ.

Reassurance

The main client was understandably concerned about the type of company purchasing Milsom and its ability to maintain the service levels and quality already established. Equally, the potential purchaser needed to feel confident that Milsom would continue to maintain its work levels and view the new owners positively, as an important partner.

A formal meeting took place to confirm the potential purchaser's commitment to the client and to clarify the client's attitude to what was clearly a substantial change in a major supplier. The outcome was reassuringly positive.

The long haul

The emotional ups and downs of the experience prompted Peter's advice for anyone selling their business: plan for the long-distance run, not for a sprint.

It wasn't just the negotiation process and the last-minute challenges from the key client that caused Peter to offer this advice, but also the workload involved in producing information. Throughout the negotiation process there are regular requests for information, and that information can be extensive, which adds significantly to the seller's workload.

Plan for the long-distance run, not for a sprint.

Maintaining confidentiality is fairly straightforward, but it too can add to the challenge. For Richard and Peter, it was sometimes difficult to explain to their staff why both directors had to disappear for meetings.

Early on in the process, they decided to take the senior accountant and a couple of managers into their confidence regarding the potential sale. Six months before the sale was finally agreed, they did the same with two more senior managers, because of issues they might face. Both directors found it difficult not to tell the people they had employed and developed over years what was happening. However, what did help was the clear decision that it served no useful purpose to worry staff before the final deal was agreed. Consequently, the main body of the staff was not informed until completion. In Peter and Richard's view this worked to everyone's advantage.

A better future

The outcome for the staff was an essential and non-negotiable element of the bidding process. Milsom's culture, reputation and reliability played an essential role in the company's relationship with all its clients, particularly its main client. Milsom's ability to respond reliably and effectively was based on the 130 technical

staff who worked on projects for this main customer. The staff effectively locked the work in. Any successful acquirer would have to demonstrate that they understood and agreed with this fact, reflecting it in any offer.

The takeover has been positive in its impact on staff. For some, there have already been slightly improved terms and conditions. What is reassuring is that the entire workforce now has a better future with the acquirer than it would have had with two directors who had reached a plateau in terms of growth and willingness to take risks.

Can you remember?

Peter's recollections of the negotiations take him to the point at which they were finally concluded, at about 4 o'clock in the morning, when a final confirmation email was received. For Peter and Richard it was almost an anticlimax. All that time invested, all the negotiation meetings, all the work done with Sunita, the deal leader from BCMS, alongside them. Then one short email and it's done and dusted, it's over.

During the days before signing, Peter was convinced they were finally getting close to something that would work well. There was a logical process going on between all involved; it was well thought out and well structured. The process was increasingly based on an intelligent mutual understanding. So it was no surprise when the final moment came.

Peter recalls having a glass of champagne with the BCMS deal leader and the lawyers, then going home for a sleep. He also recalls that he knew instinctively he could not even think about celebrating until the final minute of the final confirmation.

All change?
Earlier in the chapter, we discovered how Peter and Richard began to change in their attitudes as they took on more commitments and liabilities. Every time the business needed growth or development, the implications were personal. They had both got to the point where decision-making processes were guided by their growing aversion to personal risk rather than by the business potential. For both Peter and Richard, that pressure has been lifted totally and with immediate effect.

Knowing that the outcome has been good for the business and good for the long-term future of the staff has also added to the positive sense of relief. Financial stability means that not only is the future of the company and all the loyal staff far more secure, but also the business is now poised for a growth that Peter and Richard could not have facilitated.

An unexpected turn
When the sale was concluding, Peter's wife unexpectedly found she had to use a wheelchair. At the time no-one knew how long that was to last. As Peter said, 'It was almost as if destiny was giving me the opportunity to help her every day at a time when it

was needed.'

Thankfully Peter's wife is fine now, but it was a significant benefit to them both that Peter could be there at the right time. The children are grateful too. They've been surprised at how much Peter has been able to walk away from daily involvement, and surprised too that he's been able to give up as much as he has. Peter and the family have some great plans for overseas travel to new places in the coming few years.

With a three-year earn-out, he spent the first year post-sale working three days a week as a consultant. Now it's just 75 days a year, working from home, and going in once a week instead of every day.

'When you're running a business you're up against it all the time, but now I'm not running against the clock any more.'

The sale met Peter's financial aspirations, and financially the family's future is secure. But much more importantly for Peter, the change has made his working life a lot better. He can pace his life. As he puts it himself, 'When you're running a business you're up against it all the time, but now I'm not running against the clock any more.'

Fact file

The business

Milsom Industrial Designs operates in a niche market as a specialist technical services company working predominantly, though not exclusively, in the aerospace and defence industries.

At the time of disposal the business employed 150 staff, with a turnover of £7 million and adjusted EBIT of £487,000.

The reason for sale

The possibility of selling had been triggered by an earlier expression of interest from a potential enquirer, which ultimately came to nothing.

The main driving force was the realisation for both directors that the company had grown to a stage where any sizeable new business had a risk element. The directors were much less willing to grow another substantial part of the business, because of the financial risk to themselves.

In their view, the business was suffering from the inevitable tendency for them to play it safe and avoid risk. Both directors were crystal clear that future growth and development would require someone less risk-averse at the helm. A new owner was needed to allow the business to grow as it could.

The outcome

BCMS Corporate identified 291 potential acquirers, and 50 NDAs were signed. Ten negotiation meetings were conducted, with five firm bids received. The final deal included an earn-out period accounting for 50% of the agreed sale price and based on agreed profit targets for each of the three subsequent years.

St Annes Contractors

Would you like to buy my business?

Carl Robinson started out running his own business in the building trade, with a couple of young employees. His main client was St Annes Contractors (SAC), a painting and decorating company with a turnover of £500,000 and employing 15 people. One morning, out of the blue, the owner turned to Carl and asked a question that would change Carl's life: 'Would you like to buy this business?'

The owner had earned well from the business, was nearing retirement age and was tiring of the responsibility. He could see the energy and entrepreneurial enthusiasm in Carl, his staff liked working with Carl's team, and it seemed an obvious possibility.

From Carl's point of view, the opportunity was a mixed blessing. The company wasn't in the best state, in fact it was on its way down. He felt it had been set up to make money for the owner without any real regard for the employees; it did, however, have great structures and systems. The business focus was solely on painting and decorating, in particular working for councils and housing associations. Carl could see it had a good track record, which would enable him in time to move into bigger work. The foundations were good and could be built upon. Carl believed he had the drive and the capability to push the business forward. As he put it, 'I was confident. I had faith in myself to make it work.'

From £500,000 to £1.6 million

Carl bought the business for £40,000 on the basis of his faith in his own ability to work. At the age of 30 he had already discovered that he was wired to be his own boss. When you listen to Carl talking about work, what you hear is drive and passion. He loves getting up in the morning and can barely wait to get to work. For him, work is almost like a drug: when it's good it's like surfing the crest of a wave, the highs are so good. Carl says:

'I have always been a very driven character – as soon as I get one job I look for the next one, I push continually. That drive within me is a drive to succeed, and running my own business means I'm able to truly do it for myself and what I can get out of it.'

That confidence was well founded. By the time Carl sold the company, its turnover was £1.6 million. He'd bought the business in 1997 for £40,000 – he sold it in 2008 for more than £2 million.

Confidence tested to the brink

It's a great story, but it had its tough moments, and Carl faced some huge difficulties. In order to find the £40,000 purchase price, he began by raising some cash himself, then borrowed from friends and family, and finally borrowed £10,000 on credit cards. Everything he and his wife owned went into the purchase. As the business grew, in order to run the company he had an overdraft, secured by means of a floating charge on the business and on the value of his house. Several times Carl would say to his wife, 'If it goes bad we lose the lot, but we haven't got anything anyway.'

Carl's philosophy is that to appreciate the good times you have to go through the bad times. In the early days it was quite common for the business to be in a situation where the VAT could not be paid. They would often send the return back without the cheque, giving themselves another two or three weeks of cash flow. But it was to get more serious than that. Carl remembers the day they stood on the brink, as if it were yesterday.

It was a Wednesday morning and they had wages to pay on that Friday. The bank was owed £148,000, and there was £60,000 owing to debtors. In reality the business was trading insolvently. Carl's confidence in his ability to work his way through it was strong. There was a positive forward order book, so he called his bank manager and said simply, 'If you give me £30,000 I can turn this round, otherwise I can't pay the lads.' His bank manager said, 'The reality is you are trading insolvently, but give me till 5.30 and I will have an answer.'

Carl recalls phoning his wife to tell her the likelihood was that the business would go down that day. Her response was strong: 'I fully believe in what you're doing. If it does go down we'll stand by each other, and we'll get through it together.'

> *'If it does go down we'll stand by each other,
> and we'll get through it together.'*

The bank manager called at 5.30. She made it clear that her neck was on the block, and released the £30,000. Carl got the business into the black in nine months. The business has stayed loyal to that bank ever since!

What makes for confidence?

Every couple running a successful business sooner or later face important choices about how that relationship should work. For Carl and his wife Mary, their decision was that Carl should endeavour to leave work at work, not bring it home. In fact they would rarely even discuss the business, even though they were both shareholders. Their deliberate choice was also that Mary would provide support by looking after the home and family life. For them, this decision was to be the essence of a true partnership. For Carl, work was the driving priority: he would run life around his work. For Mary, home and family were the priority. Knowing that home and family were in a secure place fuelled Carl's confidence.

Carl's attitude to risk also helped. He believes that anyone who really wants to get on will take a gamble. For him, confidence can get eaten up if you focus on risk, and sometimes identifying too much risk can frighten you off.

Friends and colleagues would say to Carl, 'How do you know it will work?' His response was always, 'I will only look at the positives and I will make it work!'

Selling up on impulse

Carl's decision to sell was on impulse, out of the blue and unplanned. He received a promotional flyer from BCMS and sent the reply form back, thinking he would give it a go. There were no stress points, the business had been making healthy profits, and exit wasn't even a consideration until that flyer dropped on his desk.

Shortly afterwards, as he sat in the BCMS office listening to the consultant, he was already thinking, 'Let's try it.' So when the consultant said to him, 'What do you think, Carl?' his response was already decided: 'Let's give it a go then.'

Carl hadn't groomed the business for selling. By and large it had always done well, returning good profits most years. And so in the early days when he was working with BCMS to sell SAC, Carl's primary desire was to make sure his family were secure for the rest of their lives.

As the process unfolded, other factors were to increase in importance. Three offers came in which included the stipulation that Carl leave the business. However, at just 44 years of age, Carl was becoming aware that if he could stay, he might like to. He enjoyed going to work; he loved the client-facing engagement and the thrill of putting together a good deal. But – and it was a big but – Carl's drive and appetite for work, and the years he'd spent building the business himself, meant that working for someone else could prove a challenge.

The right offer
At the time of sale there was no particular pressure on Carl. He had no mortgage and had already made some useful investments. He could afford the luxury of taking time to secure the right offer. The final accepted offer contained a lump sum with staged payments, together with a retained holding (Carl still owns 20% of the shares). The lump sum gave Carl the long-term security he wanted for himself and the family. Importantly, with the new owner committed to growing the business, Carl chose to work on a full-time basis as the MD.

The relational chemistry has been critical here for both Carl and the new owner. The acquirer understood Carl's need to be left alone and given free rein. The new structure is forward-thinking. It releases Carl to be entrepreneurial and face-to-face with clients, setting up new deals. Already Carl has developed things to the point where he has become CEO of the group, with an Operations

Director taking care of day-to-day operations. There are now three companies in the group, the business has grown 35% in the past year, and the group is moving to a new office six times bigger than the current premises. For Carl these are exciting times, and something he very much wants to be part of.

The outcome is the best of all worlds: financial security for the family and exciting times again, moving a growing business forward. One huge positive for Carl has been the realisation of just how alone he had been in previous years. This has made the deal outcome even more satisfying, as he now has someone supportive alongside who understands the problems, and that of course makes it less stressful.

The right process
During the sale process, Carl found himself experiencing an unexpected mixture of mild stress and elation. Because of his perfectionism, he was committed to sticking to the process of getting the right information to all the potential buyers in a timely manner. Collating all that information and at the same time maintaining confidentiality was to become a pressure, not least because the company was doing incredibly well and he couldn't allow his focus to be diverted from successfully managing the business.

What the pressure did highlight was how good the quality assurance processes were. Information requested could be found easily and quickly, and this in turn gave prospective acquirers confidence that the systems were good.

When solicitors came in to conduct due diligence, Carl chose his moment to take four key staff into his confidence. He needed to assure them that he wasn't going anywhere. For him the big thing was to tell them the truth: that they were safe, and with bigger opportunities. The whole idea was to grow the company and enhance their careers with a potentially significant financial benefit.

Concurrently there was an unexpected emotional bonus. As

potential buyers began to value the business, the sense of achievement was bigger than the monetary valuation. Carl remembers the first offer of £3 million as a moment when it felt like someone was saying 'Well done' to all that he had achieved. For Carl it felt great to know he had achieved this on his own.

It was to be a process of self-discovery that over time would change his perceptions. Some very large potential acquirers gave feedback on how well he had done to achieve the levels of growth and profit that he had with SAC. Carl didn't realise how significant that affirmation was until he started to get it. Crucially, it alerted him to the fact that money alone should not be the determining factor in his choice of acquirer. Some form of intelligent balance in outcome was required. To achieve that, a choice of offers would be essential.

Choice of offers

One 'good' offer included the stipulation that Carl should stay in the business and 'earn out' over three years. It was an attractive deal financially, but Carl was quickly aware that he would feel hemmed in working for a big company structure. It was equally clear that he would be likely to fall out with some of the key people in the acquirer's management team, and it would not work.

> *'Choosing the wrong acquirer would have led to me losing my true identify: my entrepreneurial spirit would have been imprisoned.'*

For Carl, having the choice of offers was very important. Reflecting back on the process, he said: 'Choosing the wrong acquirer would have led to me losing my true identify: my entrepreneurial spirit would have been imprisoned.'

In the case of a handful of potential buyers, Carl was aware that he could not work with the individuals involved; the relational chemistry was simply not right. The final choice of acquirer meant a measure of risk but also freedom. For Carl it was the best of both worlds: still taking a risk, but a balanced risk. The family was totally secure financially, and Carl had the opportunity to grow something new, making the sale even more profitable over time.

In fact the potential to go through the process of growth and subsequent acquisition again was highly attractive. Carl later put it this way: 'The possibilities are exciting. In five years or so we have the very real chance of a flotation with the acquirer. I really enjoy my work, so the opportunity to grow the business with a free rein, and yet have the option of selling my shares back when I wish, is very motivating and satisfying.'

His ability to see the possibilities with the right acquirer, together with the fact that he's been given responsibility to drive those possibilities forward, means that Carl's remaining 20% will potentially end up worth more than the 80% he sold.

> *Carl's remaining 20% will potentially end up worth more than the 80% he sold.*

The right choice was also very important in terms of what it would do for the staff who had worked with Carl for years. He wanted to emphasise the importance of the key staff. It was important to him that everyone stayed. He made promises that there would be advancement for everyone, and has been able to keep his word. All the staff had bonuses at Christmas – the biggest bonus they had ever received.

Carl also wanted to tell his staff as soon as possible. The day after signing, he shared the news with the foremen and charge hands first, then half an hour later with all the staff, taking care to share the future vision of growth. The biggest positive for the staff was that he would be staying. The staff's respect and their pleasure at the fact he was staying on meant a great deal to him.

Future options

Many business owners who sell are ready to move into something less taxing, something more relaxing, something with a slower pace; a number will go into retirement.

The money from the business sale meant Carl and Mary could consider many options, and they talked this through many times in the process of selling. Carl's ultimate dream is to develop a specialised fishery with holiday accommodation set in 30 acres. It would be a comfortable living and a more relaxed lifestyle, more physically active and in the outdoors. It has a lot to commend it. But the process of selling with the BCMS team taught him that he was not ready for that more relaxed lifestyle yet. Although this realisation was a surprise for both Carl and Mary, they both know they can choose to take that path anytime they wish, from now on.

Reflections on the final moment

Waiting at the solicitors' office for the final deal confirmation, Carl found some interesting emotions surfacing. As he reflected on his personal upbringing and the origins of the business, he was deeply impacted by the realisation of where he had come from, where he had got to, and where the new business was going to take him.

The deal was also poignant for another reason: it brought back some painful memories of a time when they had nearly 'lost it all'. Some years earlier a family member had died in tragic circumstances. Carl and Mary were left comforting and supporting the rest of the family in practical ways. At the same time the business faced insolvency and was close to going under. The shock of it all was to cause the onset of diabetes for Carl.

For Carl, this day was to change all that and heal some of those painful memories. It was a day that would give him a real sense of achievement, providing security for his family and the assurance that the roof over their heads would never be at risk again. They had been through and achieved a lot, but Carl and Mary decided against an extravagant celebration. Instead they went home and had tea with their two children in quiet satisfaction.

Fact file

The business
St Annes Contractors (SAC) operates as a painting, decorating, building, refurbishment and repair contractor. The business was grown from £500,000 to £1.6 million at the time of sale, with a profit before tax of £349,000.

The reason for sale
The owner's decision to sell was on impulse, out of the blue and unplanned. He received a promotional flyer from BCMS and sent the reply form back, thinking he would give it a go. There were no stress points, the business had been making healthy profits, and exit wasn't even a consideration until the flyer landed on his desk!

The outcome
BCMS Corporate identified more than 250 potential acquirers; 49 signed an NDA, and three entered the formal negotiation process.

The owner wanted to continue working and has retained a 20% share in the new business. The deal releases him to be entrepreneurial and to work face-to-face with clients, setting up new deals. Already things have developed to the point where he has become CEO of the group, with an Operations Director taking care of day-to-day operations. That retained shareholding of 20% will potentially end up worth more than the 80% originally sold: a doubly good outcome.

There are now three companies in the acquiring group, the business grew 35% in the past year, and the group is moving to a new office six times bigger than its current premises.

EMC Advisory Services

An Indian takeaway in Torquay

EMC began when a syndicate approached Nick Hamlet and Graham Lafbery, looking for endowment mortgage customers who might have been mis-advised. Graham and Nick both had marketing backgrounds and quickly acquired vast numbers of clients. Early into the project, the syndicate pulled away, leaving Graham and Nick with a large client base requiring help.

Graham asked his brother-in-law Adrian Devine for strategic input and practical advice in handling the unexpectedly large volume. Adrian suggested they meet with companies operating in the same industry who might be able to take on these clients.

They found a company working in endowments that was confident it could handle the existing clients together with any new business. In the previous two years this company had secured 1,000 clients, whereas the EMC team was securing the same number of new customers each month! The decision was therefore taken, with the appropriate changes in the business model, to take on the claims handling as well as the new client generation.

Within the first six months, working from just one room, they had seen the first award in favour of a client, had moved ahead of the business plan, and had already repaid their first business loan. The three owners met in a dimly lit room above an Indian takeaway in Torquay, with a whiteboard for equipment, and began to rewrite the business plan! As the business grew, it expanded next door into some rooms in a government building for job seekers. After further growth they took on another office, then they outgrew that and moved to the current premises in Paignton, Devon.

Adrian remembers the symptoms of growth. He had taken some business introducers out for an evening thank-you meal, and on the way back from the restaurant they passed the office entrance. Through the glass door they could see that the floor was covered with letters. The postman claimed that the mail coming in to the company was too heavy for the sack, so a van was used to deliver it, and finally the business got its own postcode.

The team of three grew, and each found his role expanding as new skills and responsibilities emerged. Nick and Graham naturally continued with lead generation. Nick's responsibilities expanded into IT, and Graham's into HR and staffing. Adrian provided part-time input on financial and general management issues. Within a year the firm had grown at such a pace that Adrian joined the team full time.

Bollinger moments

The team learned to work hard and play hard. They had plenty of Bollinger moments, times to celebrate together for achieving the business plan and with customers who won awards.

The team was regularly winning money for people. Letters of appreciation arrived in phenomenal volumes, thanking the business for the outcomes achieved, many of which had changed people's lives. Adrian recalled one particular letter from an elderly lady whose husband could retire early on the basis of the result EMC had achieved.

Every summer the business would host events such as a murder mystery in an old manor house overlooking Salcombe Bay. 'It's a Knockout' was another favourite, offering a chance for owners and staff to relax and have fun together. In time EMC became the second largest employer in the Torbay area. There were lots of positive, motivating reasons for enjoying the business.

In comparison with many businesses of a similar size, the stress levels were remarkably low. Occasionally Graham and Nick would find regulations relating to IT and HR a little stressful, particularly as the headcount grew. However, even though the managers were not soft, business growth targets were set at a realistic level and were surpassed every year. Stress was not a primary reason to consider a sale.

Stress was not a primary reason to consider a sale.

A different M&A philosophy

Adrian had a finance and M&A background and was convinced that any disposal activity for EMC would require something different. He knew that a traditional approach would not work; a different style would be required. It would need the right person or organisation, capable of thinking out of the box.

The team had been thinking about their future and discussing options when they received a promotional flyer from BCMS. Adrian's view was simple: there was nothing to lose by having an initial conversation with a BCMS consultant. From the team's point of view, the process would give some idea of valuation and provide a safe way of finding out whether Nick and Graham could achieve any desired outcomes from an exit.

A decision to sell

Both Nick and Graham had worked hard. Their ambition had always been to run a successful business. Having achieved that, they felt they could explore the possibility of selling, provided the business and its staff could be left in safe hands. For all three the business and its staff were an important consideration, along with the firms that had worked with them from the beginning.

As with any business sale, personal aspirations also featured. As well as protecting the business and its staff, the sale had to realise enough money to enable financial independence. Each of the three had to make a different calculation to match their desired outcomes.

Thoughts on the journey

Selling was one attractive option, but only if the right price could be achieved. All three shareholders were earning significant sums each year. There was no financial pressure to sell, and there was no financial angst in the mix. In fact the business had always been cash rich. This meant that a sale was not the only option.

If the business could not be sold, it would be an opportunity to consider producing a new business plan, and a good time to bring in a new management team with a new finance director and managing director. At the same time this enabled the three to explore the possibility of stepping back from day-to-day responsibilities – making time available for other things.

A major concern for the team was people. As Adrian put it, 'We wanted to be certain that we looked after our key staff and our business introducers. They had helped us grow this business, and we didn't want them thinking they'd been left out in the cold. Any deal we accepted had to be good for them too.'

As they began to produce forward-looking business plans, a question would often surface in their minds: What if? What if the new acquirers can't run this as well as we do? What if they make decisions that negatively affect the core values we've built up over years?

Frustrations emerge

The sale of EMC took a few twists and turns, mainly because of the continuing international banking crisis and legislative changes. On that long journey, from time to time Adrian would feel frustrated, especially when deals didn't materialise because of the banking community's general reluctance to fund. An EBIT of up to 50% is bound to generate interest, but not always from the right sources. Adrian recalls working with Simon, Rob and Andy from BCMS on the business plan, the future-casts, and all the key data for a would-be acquirer. He later recalled: 'That team of three did a great job, and one of their tough challenges on our behalf was that we were a new company in a newly emerging market. New regulations made the process even more complex, as potential acquirers struggled to fully understand the environment in which EMC operated.'

The experience caused the team to rethink who the potential acquirers might be. The possibility of an overseas company was revisited, as was the equity route. Because of the newly appointed EMC management team, BCMS was able to generate a good level of interest from the private equity community. Numerous meetings were arranged at which this new team presented. Offers resulted, but because EMC's services included claiming against banks, funding the transaction was inevitably difficult. Another round of frustration and disappointment.

Forward impetus

With the MBO as a preferred option, Catalyst Partners was brought in to work alongside the new management team, supporting them at meetings with private equity firms. The company was also tasked with arranging the specialist finance. This process went extremely well and led to bids from a number of equity firms, including Lonsdale. After meetings with those bidders, Lonsdale emerged as the one most likely to maintain the EMC core values, providing the right level of support for the management team and their future development.

As the project neared the finishing line, another legislative challenge impacted one of the EMC products. A court case ensued, and with it an uncertain outcome. At first glance it looked as if the process would be thwarted yet again. However, the relationship with Lonsdale had developed so well that the team felt confident they could restructure the deal, with the vendors providing a significant proportion of the funding.

On the basis of this solution the deal was concluded fairly quickly.

Three different outcomes
At the same time, as if this process were not difficult enough, the involvement of three shareholders, each with their own 'desired outcome', led to parallel challenges. The team had 'interesting' conversations, where a potential deal would achieve one person's desired outcome but not achieve that number for the other two. Understandably, this put pressure on the process and on the three shareholders.

Eventually these discussions reached clear agreement on the minimum value that would enable each of them to achieve their desired outcomes. Adrian put it this way: 'You have to stay detached: if you're all clear on the value of the business, you stick to it. If you believe that's what it's worth, don't give it away for less. That way, if the offer is not in the right ballpark you can walk away.'

'If you're all clear on the value of the business, you stick to it. If you believe that's what it's worth, don't give it away for less.'

When it came to negotiating positions, it became difficult for all three to have the same resilience in holding their corporate nerve for what was deemed to be a fair price. For that reason, by agreement, Adrian would act as team leader in the negotiations. Several times the team had to stay firm and renegotiate the process, and several times Adrian himself called deals off.

Points of impact

The average deal at BCMS Corporate takes between nine and 12 months, but this one took longer. The team of three had to make some choices early on, as it became apparent that the sale might take a while. They determined that they wouldn't do anything differently while the sale process was being explored; they continued to grow the business as they always had. Questions arose as they looked at ways to develop new strategies. What if this decision affects profitability and cash holdings in the short term? How will that then impact any sale?

In the meantime, however, these questions and the protracted sale process were not allowed to interfere with the continued running of the business and its development.

Handling the staff

All along, the well-being of staff and introducers was a high priority. Shortly after the deal completion, the team was involved in crafting what was said and how it was to be communicated to the staff. On behalf of the team, Adrian also went to a meeting with the lead introducers to explain the transaction.

Nick and Graham took the long-serving staff out for a thank-you meal and had a very moving evening, with a number in tears. For Nick and Graham, who were continuing to live in Torquay, where so many of their staff lived, it was particularly important that there be goodwill at exit.

Celebrating the deal with Joan Collins

When it came to the final completion of the deal, Nick and Graham were on holiday. Together with his wife Sharon, Adrian and the BCMS team were with their lawyer Mark Hodge at his Birmingham offices. The plan was to sign up and then have a quiet evening celebrating together. Mark supplied some champagne, and it was only when that was drunk that the other side finally signed! Time to celebrate properly, on what was to become an unexpectedly memorable occasion.

As they sat down for dinner together at the Post Box restaurant in Birmingham, Adrian leaned over to BCMS's Andy and said, 'Don't make it too conspicuous, but Joan Collins is sitting just behind you.' Trying hard to make it inconspicuous, Andy took a look, and sure enough the famous actress was indeed sitting at a table close by. Urged on by the team, Andy went across to her table, explained what they were celebrating, and asked if she might be willing for a photograph together.

As Adrian put it, 'The celebration was great, but behind it lay a journey with significant frustrations en route. I never expected it to take as long as it did, and as the evening continued it seemed appropriate to give team leader Andy a thank-you hug. Andy had hung in there for the entire journey and despite the twists and turns had remained very professional and committed.'

Outcomes for the shareholders
As we saw earlier in this chapter, each of the shareholders had a desired outcome related to their life goals post-sale, and their final choices reflected this.

> *Each of the shareholders had a desired outcome related to their life goals post-sale, and their final choices reflected this.*

Adrian has enjoyed his share of holidays and so is ready for a new challenge; he misses the buzz of entrepreneurial activity. In his mind he wrestles with a personal question related to the success of EMC: 'Were we lucky or were we great?' Some form of new entrepreneurial activity beckons.

With a new management team in place, things had already begun to change positively for the family, and now of course that is even more the case. As Adrian reflected on the past few years, he conceded that in common with most of us he had spent years at the beck and call of the company. As he put it, 'Running a successful business doesn't always do a lot for family life. There comes a point where you know you have to get your priorities right. Most important are family, friends and health, then after that comes money.'

> *'Most important are family, friends and health, then after that comes money.'*

Sharon loves it that Adrian is around more and able to have a conversation without picking up emails or texting on his Blackberry. For her and the two children, having a meal without Dad stepping outside for a call, or having a car journey with the Bluetooth switched off, has made a difference. The children have had different reactions to the sale. Both have been delighted to have more time with Dad. Both have expressed concern, as he now has time to drop them off to school: 'What are you doing today? Aren't you going to work?'

Adrian's daughter Danielle likes to tease Dad: 'You're not giving my inheritance away, are you?' Craig's concern is more pragmatic: 'Who's going to pay you now, Dad? Where will your money come from?'

Graham initially spent time out of the country on holidays. Subsequently he has bought a great house overlooking the harbour, where he can keep a good eye on his newly acquired boat. He increasingly has more time to spend at sea.

Nick is enjoying more time with his partner and friends and has also been able to take a good number of holidays. In his case his holidays have given him time to reflect, ponder and prepare for his next ventures.

All three are delighted with their outcomes.

Fact file

The business

EMC provides a claims management service to consumers seeking compensation, in the main from large financial institutions which may have mis-sold products such as endowment mortgages or payment protection insurance as well as overcharging on credit card charges.

At the time of sale the turnover was £17.5 million, with an EBIT of up to 50%. The purchaser was a Lonsdale private equity-backed MBO.

The reason for sale

The three had been thinking about and discussing options for their future when they received a promotional flyer from BCMS Corporate.

Adrian Devine's view was simple: there was nothing to lose by having an initial consultation with a BCMS consultant.

From the team's point of view the process would give some idea of valuation and provide a safe way of finding out whether the shareholders could achieve their desired outcomes from an exit.

The outcome

91 potential acquirers were identified and 49 NDAs signed. 23 negotiation meetings were held, with six offers made.

All three shareholders exceeded their aspirations regarding the sale, have achieved their desired outcome, and are living out their chosen future.

ANTECH ENGINEERING

Taking an opportunity

Jim Gunn and Ron McDonald have been friends since 1976, working together in different oil and gas related companies in a variety of roles, including overseas assignments. From time to time they had remarked to each other that if ever the opportunity to start their own business presented itself, they would quite like to take it.

During his last year as manager in a Great Yarmouth based company, Ron identified a market in testing services that wasn't being supplied. He contacted Jim, who didn't take much persuasion, and within a week Antech Engineering was formed.

The business opportunity that the pair had identified was rental of test and measuring equipment to offshore oil and gas facilities and construction companies that supported the industry in the southern North Sea. At that time there were six or seven large players in the area that could use this kind of service.

Together from the start

Both Jim and Ron had worked in the Far East and accumulated a reasonable amount of capital; this, together with mortgages raised on their houses, enabled them to buy the initial stock of test equipment. To keep the cash flow going for the newly started company, Jim continued working locally on contract to Shell. Ron took on full-time responsibilities running the new start-up, and in the evening Jim would help out, calibrating equipment and handling the paperwork. Inevitably there were long hours, and the pair would usually stop for an 'unwinder' before going home. In those early days it was particularly hard work, only possible thanks to their highly supportive families.

Ron remained Antech's sole employee for six months. From day one there was demand for their services, and their extensive network of relationships and personal contacts meant that work flowed well. Antech quickly gained a reputation for its standard of equipment and quality of service. The substantial early investment needed meant there was no cash in the business: Jim's contract income paid Ron's wages. To keep costs to a minimum, they rented some inexpensive first-floor space from the local council. Everything had to be carried up a flight of stairs: an office to the left, a workshop to the right, not exactly ideal, but as they say elsewhere, 'Every little helps.'

One of the things that helped them to get established in those early months was when an Aberdeen-based company offered to sell its assets. Purchasing these allowed Antech to move ahead into other areas of rental. All this, together with other growth pains and the hiring of the first employee, meant it was more than a year before Jim could begin to earn income directly from the business.

Piper Alpha – tragic but influential
The business continued to attract attention in the locality, partly because of its reputation but also because Antech was one of only two companies offering these specific services. And in a strange twist of history, Antech was also to find itself growing as a result of someone else's misfortune.

The Piper Alpha oil rig disaster of 1988, in which an explosion and fire claimed 167 lives, led to a sudden and large-scale requirement for testing equipment and services for safety provision. Ron and Jim's experience gave them a unique insight into what would be required, and they were able to gear the business towards serving that requirement. The Cullen Inquiry reported in 1990, making numerous recommendations requiring the offshore industry to upgrade its facilities. One of the southern North Sea companies won a large contract, and as a direct result Antech was engaged to supply all the test equipment for it. In a new and unexpected development, they were also asked to supply personnel: instrumentation engineers, technicians and pipe fitters.

Cash flow was brilliant, with Antech invoicing good sums each month and getting paid on time, but the new requirement for supply of personnel was to be taxing in quite a different way.

I would sooner run a kindergarten!

Ron and Jim recall this phase with mixed emotions. It was all very memorable, very positive and full of mainly positive growth. In fact the growth had been virtually continuous, with profitable rental income increasing, allowing investment into other areas. But as Ron was to discover, the newly acquired opportunity to supply personnel would entail its own cost.

Jim's responsibilities included payroll, customer service and administrative functions. Ron was now tasked with finding and recruiting personnel and then deploying them offshore. Looking back at this period in the business history, Ron remarked, 'It would have been easier to run a kindergarten than to recruit, deploy and manage offshore personnel'.

'For a young company we had a large workforce, simply because there was an opportunity to be had. But personnel supply was a management nightmare: individuals were unreliable, and the business suffered all the kickbacks of employing people who work hard offshore and then play hard onshore. We only stayed in personnel supply for nine months.'

Other companies were far better geared to do this than Antech. The experiment was distracting, and for Ron and Jim it was time to get back to doing what they did best.

Doing what we do best

The decision to pull out of supplying personnel and focus on rental was to open another very significant door. As part of the quality processes associated with rental equipment, every piece of kit that goes out of the door requires formal acknowledgement

and certification confirming that it is fit for purpose. As this became an ingrained internal process, Antech found itself drawn into the calibration market. As Ron put it, 'Calibrating our own equipment taught us that was the way we wanted to go.'

This was to prove serendipitous. A significant number of construction companies were leaving the Great Yarmouth area, and inevitably there was no longer the same requirement for rental services. As more competitive companies from Aberdeen were competing for these reduced rental opportunities, the decision was made to shift into calibration with an ISO 9002 capability.

From their earlier employment with exploration companies, both Ron and Jim had a background in fiscal metering, a high-profile, technically complex service in high demand. They therefore decided to establish a UK Accreditation Service (UKAS) accredited laboratory in the East of England. They made the investment decision to buy land and create a purpose-built laboratory.

Jim summarised the attitude he and Ron espoused: 'Our vision was to move forward, and our mantra was "Putting money back in is the way to move forward." In our industry, to move forward you simply have to invest. We used to sit down and discuss where the opportunity was and what we needed to spend, and then determine if we could afford it! If we thought we could, we would quickly make the decision and go for it.'

He remembers one experience ruefully: 'We made an investment to go into an area. Shortly afterwards the client company was bought out and subsequently took the work back in house. Most of our investments worked out well, however, and there was good support from the banks in those days. In hindsight we both think we could have been even more adventurous.'

This kind of regular investment is often a strain on small business partnerships, but somehow for Ron and Jim it was never that kind of challenge. Jim says, 'We've always chosen to share an office and have built the business with close communication every day. Continuing to share an office meant we were never physically isolated. We were both aware of everything, aware of what was happening in each other's realms of responsibility. It made running the business a little easier, and it also made investment decisions easier: they were simply an extension of what we were talking about naturally during an ordinary day.'

Unsolicited approaches open a door

During 2008 and 2009 Antech had a couple of unexpected approaches from blue chip companies, with formal offers made. The process unsurprisingly got Ron and Jim thinking: if offers had come so easily and unsolicited, it was fair to assume there might be many more potential acquirers with deeper pockets.

Both men were approaching the big '60', and they needed to figure out the future of the business. They agreed that they needed to start planning properly for their retirement. Work was still interesting, but some parts of the work, especially HR and the growing compliance paperwork, were getting more complex and more bureaucratic. Neither of them was especially comfortable in these areas.

Ron describes it like this: 'We needed someone to grow the business. We had reached the capacity of our personal time and energy levels. The business needed more, and we were already maxed out. We didn't want to get on a plane again.'

'We had reached the capacity of our personal time and energy levels. The business needed more and we were already maxed out. We didn't want to get on a plane again.'

Another factor influencing the potential exit was the prospect of growing competition on the horizon. Jim and Ron were aware that Antech was a relatively small fish, albeit with a great reputation. There were bigger organisations which were growing fast, and they began to think that maybe Antech's future would be best served if it were acquired by one of these larger organisations, which could then preserve and grow the good things Antech had to offer.

They began this pursuit with their accountants, a very reputable firm that had been with them since day one. Antech engaged them to help sell the company. They did okay, but as Ron put it, 'Our accountants weren't marketing people: they were still accountants. We have no complaints about what they did, but we didn't feel they were pushing it. We gave them names of firms that might be interested, but it didn't seem to be getting anywhere. I thought: these accountants are asking us to provide a list, so they can sell to it. We quickly realised they didn't have the resources or the skills to do the job in the way we needed it done.'

'Our accountants weren't marketing people. We have no complaints about what they did, but we quickly realised they didn't have the resources to do this job in the way we needed it done.'

A brochure opens the door wider

When a BCMS promotional flyer arrived, both Ron and Jim were keen to attend the seminar. Speaking with one of the presenters at the end of the presentation, they made the decision to engage BCMS to market the business properly. As Jim put it, 'It didn't take a lot of thinking about: here's a company with a good record that seem highly likely to be able to maximise the value of our business. Certainly their active marketing is likely to achieve more than the accountancy firm could do.

'With BCMS we were confident we had found the right concept and the right system. We liked the distance between the potential suitors and us; we felt very comfortable with that. We soon realised there are stresses and strains in negotiation positions and everyone has to feel happy. The acquirer wants to feel they paid the right price, and as the seller we also wanted to be sure we had got the best possible price and terms. Doubly difficult, because in our case we knew we needed to work together afterwards. We would not have achieved this without the BCMS process.'

From Jim's perspective the process was well structured and not too intrusive. The hardest part was getting the IM together. It took a lot of effort and needed to be accurate, with BCMS rightly pushing to get it completed. It made both Jim and Ron think a lot about the business too, and from their standpoint it was a great discipline to go through, because it got them back in 'close touch' with the performance of the company, getting the numbers and the forecasts right, which would in turn be critical to the process. Interestingly, the process had the effect of building their belief and confidence in the value of the business and its attractiveness to a potential acquirer.

> *'With BCMS we were confident we had found the right concept and the right system.'*

Keeping the potential sale a secret was an unexpected stress trigger! During the due diligence process the deal is never a foregone conclusion, and yet a lot of information is needed. Staff have to be involved in providing that information, and it's normal and inevitable for staff to get curious. With two-way confidentiality agreements in place, keeping the process under wraps can take some careful management.

Retirement wasn't the primary driver

Antech was successful and generating good profits for both Ron and Jim, providing them both with a good lifestyle. Their main focus now was to get a good price for the company and to secure the future for both the business and the staff. As Jim explained, 'In many ways this business was all about the people we employed. Antech would have been nothing without the calibre of its people, and they deserved another 10–15 good years. We could have run the business down and in theory made more money, but it wouldn't have grown. It was time to let fresh finance and fresh management in to take Antech to the next step.'

Tense moments at the last

Jim described the final deal process as a series of expectations raised, followed by anticlimaxes that knocked things back.

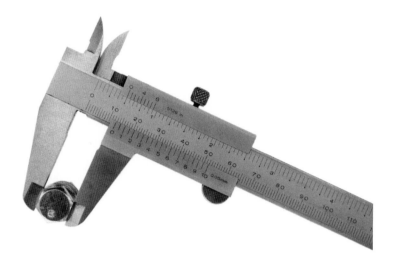

The final deal was done in central London. Jim was attending a family wedding in Canada and couldn't be there. Ron was in attendance on his own, the only time Jim and he had been apart for an important moment in the business.

For Ron the sense of 'theatre' in the lawyers' office was quite interesting: the drama, the snags, and the potential deal-breaking 'Oh no!' moments. He recalls the scene vividly: 'Purchasers were at one end of the room, solicitors and BCMS in the middle, with just me at the other end. The intensity of the atmosphere was so strong it felt as if it could be cut with a knife. The solicitors seemed to be forever fishing for issues. The acquirer would counter by looking for specific compromises. Suddenly the realisation dawned that the process was running out of time to meet the banks' ability to deal with the financial transactions. Both sides had been trying to achieve an outcome from 9.30 in the morning till 3.15 in the afternoon. Fortunately they eventually agreed – with only a few minutes to spare!'

Ron remarked, 'We used the lawyers recommended by BCMS,

and it was an utter relief. They had obviously worked with BCMS before and were well practised in working together, so it eased the way forward. Antech's own accountants looked after the financials.

> *'We used the lawyers recommended by BCMS, and it was an utter relief, so it eased the way forward.'*

'Having BCMS involved meant multiple offers. At the very last minute we had an unexpected and upwardly revised offer by email from one firm. However, we didn't sell Antech to the highest bidder: we sold to the company we felt confident would stick to their word going forward.'

The first phone call to Jim was at 4am in the North Hero House, a historic inn in Vermont. Jim was due to be driving to Montreal, so there was no celebration, and an added complication was that the company employed his son. Over breakfast Jim found himself telling his own son that he would be working for new employers! It just had to be that way.

When the deal was finally concluded, the BCMS team and the solicitors, together with Ron and his wife, had a few glasses of wine. Ron called Jim to confirm the deal was done, and they reminisced for some moments, then the anticlimax settled like a layer of low grey cloud both for Ron on his way back to Great Yarmouth and for Jim on his drive to Montreal.

Neither Ron nor Jim had a real celebration on the day, but in time the acquirers hosted an exceptionally pleasant meal with the whole team from their side and Jim and Ron and their wives. As some time had elapsed, this seemed appropriate and was an enjoyable occasion for all four.

Surprise bereavement with no regrets

As with other business owners featured in this book, for both Ron and Jim the main emotion was not euphoria but anticlimax. Ron describes it like this: 'Suddenly, with one signature, this baby that's been yours for 22 years is gone, and you don't really know for sure where it's going. Inevitably you begin to ask yourself: have I done the right thing?' The tense nature of the final deal session builds to an emotional crescendo. Like most other sellers, at this point Ron and Jim found it hard to cut away and relax.

One surprise for Jim was the sense of something like bereavement as the final deal was concluded and life without his 'Antech baby' loomed large. As a keen pilot, Jim has to take an annual aeronautical fitness exam. His doctor – an aeronautical examiner – asked him if he'd had any major life changes in the past year. When Jim related the sale of the business, the next question took him by surprise: 'Have you had depressions or feelings of depression since?'

As Jim said, 'The question helped in a way, as I realised these feelings of loss were well documented by medics. That fact helped me to more clearly understand the nature of the emotional challenge.'

A good future?

Ron has worked since he was 16 and is ready for a well-earned retirement. As he admits, 'I haven't stayed awake a single night since the sale. I'm going out regularly to play some golf, spending time with the grandchildren and enjoying some family time, and I will take at least three months' sabbatical to see what emerges.'

Jim has decided that he wants to stay on and continue working at Antech for a period yet to be determined. He has been pleasantly surprised by the experience to date, although he confesses to finding big company reporting and management information processes somewhat tedious.

Both Ron and Jim are delighted with the acquirer, Trescal. All the staff have stayed, which was one of the outcomes Ron and Jim had especially wanted. Also pleasing is the fact that Antech has not been rebranded. They both feel that is objective testimony to the quality of the business and its reputation.

Fact file

The business

Antech Calibration Services is a leading instrumentation, calibration and engineering laboratory which utilises extensive in-house testing facilities to provide UKAS-accredited and traceable calibration services across a wide spectrum of parameters.

The reason for sale

Directors Jim Gunn and Ron McDonald had received a number of unsolicited approaches, which made them aware that a sale could be possible. This in turn led to a strategic decision. They both felt they had reached the limits of their individual time and energy and were convinced that for the good of the business they should consider a sale to an acquirer who could develop the many opportunities for growth and build on the foundation they had laid.

The outcome

A total of 284 companies were identified as prospective acquirers, and 28 NDAs were signed. Eighteen companies entered the negotiative dialogue, with 10 offers submitted.

The eventual acquirer was Trescal SA, a world-leading calibration services company headquartered in France and operating 57 laboratories with sales in 2011 of £132 million.

Attainment Matters

A unique niche business

ATMA specialises in providing outsourced professional services to business networks, trade associations, charities and membership bodies, all of which operate in the non-profit sector. But importantly, ATMA brings a commercial understanding to that sector: ATMA's skills complement those of its clients, providing them with the commercial edge needed to help them prosper.

ATMA offers a range of services, from the basics of accounting and database management through to full secretariat provision: coordinating professional services to members by running their committees, managing research and publications, representing the organisation in relevant areas of public policy, putting on events - large and small - and arranging comprehensive communication to members, supporters and the public at large, including effective PR coverage and web presence.

This kind of business is very hands-on in its approach: a high degree of personal involvement is necessary, and responsibility for defined outcomes and fulfilment lies at the heart of its success. A typical client would be the Urban Place Management Association (UPMA), which includes property owners, developers, local authorities, public-private town centre management partnerships, retailers, architects and consultants. This is a sizeable association, where the common interest is an involvement in town centres but where the specific interests of each member are varied. The association embraces a multitude of stakeholders and service providers, with ultimate benefit also to the local communities, businesses and users of town centres.

Working together

The two founding directors of ATMA were Alf Tanner and Mark Taylor. Alf ran a large regional electronic security business in the

1980s, with Mark joining in 1986. The complementary skill set, and their close hard-working business relationship during those early years, was to set the scene for the later formation of ATMA.

The emergence of CCTV monitoring in town centres provided an opening for Alf to become a founder board member of UPMA. His strength as a commercial leader was recognised at an early stage and he became increasingly involved in the organisation in a voluntary capacity. Dependent entirely on skeleton staffing, volunteer board member input and goodwill, the association was self-limiting. With this in mind, its board decided to put the organisation on a more solid footing. Alf and Mark set up ATMA, and UPMA became its first client.

Alf was always an inveterate networker. With retail being the major contributor to the success of the town centre, Alf had started to establish relationships with the major shopping centre owners and operators. This drew Alf towards the Retail Property Federation (RPF), which liked the look of ATMA's capability and Alf and Mark's commercial rationale. It too bought in to the concept and transferred its secretariat contract to ATMA.

In the very early days the business comprised Alf, Mark and one staff member. Alf and Mark were already absorbed in organising ATMA's first major event: the First World Congress in Urban Place Management for UPMA. They very quickly learned the technique of outsourcing both routine and specialist skills, while establishing a core staff team of three others within the first three months.

Different ages, different roles
At the time, Mark was 40 and Alf 13 years his senior. Their roles were completely different. From the beginning Alf's background and skills meant he would take the lead role, networking, influencing and outward-facing. Mark took care of delivery, finance, database and operations management.

The role for ATMA was pretty clear. Run the association, deliver the association's services, and grow the association. Mark put it this way: 'We survived and prospered because we did a great job. Our clients were typically "make it happen" board members, doing this job voluntarily but accustomed to having dependable resources in their own organisations. We could implement a self-funding business plan to grow their association, and in the process deliver a great service to its members. They would inevitably be well pleased.'

ATMA quickly built a great track record of generating members and achieving large numbers for conference attendance. The skill in the business enabled the team to get to grips with what an association needed in order to grow: subscriptions, events, communications and infrastructure. By increasing the value and appeal of membership and involvement, they would inevitably see subscriptions grow and engage more corporate donors. The business model was pretty simple at this point: as they grew each client association, their own business grew and they became more and more embedded in the client organisation. It was a win/win that could potentially be replicated.

Energy and fulfilment
In common with many small business owners, Alf and Mark enjoyed the adventure and success of the early years. As Mark recalls, 'We understood what was needed for the client, and we knew it would take long hours and enthusiastic hands-on involvement to get the right results.'

In the early days, with just the two of them as the key players and their Westminster office base, Alf and Mark both worked away from home, putting in 'silly' hours. It would become quite normal for them to call a halt at 6pm, work out at a local gym, then have a quick Chinese meal together before returning to work, often until 11pm.

Alf and Mark really enjoyed the sense of purpose and the

successful outcomes they were achieving for their clients. Clients were very appreciative, and the difference ATMA could make was measurable. RPF grew from an income of less than £500,000 to £1.5 million in only three years. Subscriptions grew, and events attendance was outstanding, soon attracting more than 1,000 delegates to the annual conference. UPMA went stellar in terms of its international recognition as a leading authority on urban place management.

These were days of heady, fulfilling success, fuelled by a great working relationship, but Alf and Mark were increasingly conscious that they were building value for their clients, not for themselves. While doing a great job for their first two clients, Alf and Mark realised that there was a real business development opportunity for them here. Eventually the penny dropped: their own business should also be developed.

With a renewed focus on broadening their own client base, over a period of a few years they grew to 10 clients looked after by 20 members of staff. ATMA began to enjoy the benefits of scale and scope. The growing number of clients, in time, enabled ATMA to take on really high-quality staff, and the workload development became shouldered by a growing team, hungry for responsibility.

Different ages, different futures

In 2007 new possibilities emerged. As the majority shareholder, and also somewhat older than Mark, Alf had independently begun to think about retirement and the possibility of selling the business. A board member of one of their clients was with a firm of accountants which had a corporate finance arm. In the process of 'testing the water' Alf went to talk to them about the possibility of a merger. The result was an 'offer', according to which the acquirer would take 100% of the business, giving Alf and Mark £150,000 less than they could earn from it themselves over three years! Not a very attractive proposition.

During this period BCMS promotional flyers had been dropping on the doormat. Alf responded and attended a seminar. Positively impacted by what he heard, he encouraged Mark to visit a subsequent event together with him. Ultimately they agreed to appoint BCMS to sell the business in January 2008.

Both Mark and Alf were aware that ATMA was vulnerable with its relatively small client base. Some kind of step change was needed to retain existing clients and also to develop new ones. The business was at a stage where it needed more finance and resources than they had to move it forward.

The business was at a stage where it needed more finance and resources than they had to move it forward.

Mark remembers a regular comment from Alf: 'I wish I was 10 years younger!' Personal health too became an important ingredient in the mix. Alf had had bypass surgery some years previously, and he was receiving follow-up treatment. Alf, whose wife Natalie also had a lead role in the business, had two young children that he wanted to spend more time with.

What Alf and Mark discovered at this time was that they each had different motivations to achieve the same end. Partly because of his proximity to retirement age, Alf did not feel he could take ATMA to its next level. Mark was keen to explore change and didn't want to develop the business without Alf alongside. Mark commented, 'Alf was approaching retirement age, and I was at a life stage where I wanted to have a crack at another career. We both wanted the best for the business too, and I suppose our joint rationale was: let's see if someone else can take this on and develop it further.'

Mark's wife Lynn was positive about the possibilities. Aware that her husband was ready for a career change, she saw an exit as providing some financial security and perhaps opening up the opportunity for something different.

Dilemmas and concerns

Because of the very small client base, both directors felt particularly vulnerable to any possible 'leaks of information'. Preserving confidentiality was therefore very high on the agenda.

As Mark expressed it, 'Confidentially was a big fear at first in our minds, but very quickly the way we and BCMS worked meant it didn't prove to be an issue.'

> *'Confidentially was a big fear at first in our minds,*
> *but very quickly the way we and BCMS worked*
> *meant it didn't prove to be an issue.'*

As a minority shareholder, Mark was faced with a personal challenge too. At just 50 years of age, the thought of taking some finance from the deal was attractive, but the inevitable question raised was: will the deal provide me with enough? And if not, will I get a job of the right kind at my age?

The expectation was that both men would exit the business at the same time, and the hope was that the right new buyer would want some significant input. Neither man wanted an earn-out that would be large in terms of percentage of the total deal agreed, but both wanted to contribute and play a part in the new future. Since Mark and Alf knew where the business was capable of going, they also believed they knew how best to help any new owner get the business there.

ATMA had split functions in two locations: back office and administration in rural Derbyshire and front-end services in London. Concern for the staff in these two offices was an important issue. At the time of any new appointment, Mark and Alf had taken great care to ensure that they employed the best people available in terms of ability. Providing a safe and certain future for these staff became a significant part of the negotiation dialogue. Concern was especially strong for the staff in Derbyshire, who would be less likely to find equivalent jobs if the new acquirer did not retain them.

An unfounded scepticism
Mark's skill set, as we have seen, is systemisation and project management, so he rose to the challenge. The sale of the business became his responsibility and his project. Although the BCMS

team undertook the majority of the work, on occasions Mark found the process quite time-consuming, especially at the stage of due diligence.

Mark assessed the potential buyers provided by BCMS and took responsibility for preparing for the negotiations, keeping Alf briefed all the way through.

Mark remembers being quite sceptical. As he put it, 'Having attended a seminar in the summer of 2007, both Alf and I were sceptical about the BCMS numbers. At the seminar we were told that on average BCMS locates some 200 potential acquirers, and that the difference between lowest and highest bids averages 2½ times. We were also told that the average sale achieves 40% above traditional valuations.

> *'Both Alf and I were sceptical*
> *about the BCMS numbers.'*

'The processes seemed to run like clockwork, and the numbers worked out almost exactly as promised. We had 184 prospects identified after agreeing the research strategy together. The BCMS Prospect Generation Team then produced 26 signed NDAs, resulting ultimately in four prospects in negotiative dialogue.'

> *'The numbers worked out almost exactly as promised.*
> *We had 184 prospective acquirers identified.'*

The importance of different types of acquirer

Four serious bidders entered the final negotiation phases. The mix of firms was important. As expected, there was interest from a US company in a similar business. This company already had a European office in Brussels and wanted a UK presence. There was a UK competitor, and a related business focused on events. At first glance, the events management company seemed a

reasonable fit, as 50% of ATMA income is generated from events.

There was also an outsider, a 'wild card', in the form of a business process outsourcer called Empalert. This potential acquirer was in the business of consumer contact and communications services in the areas of health and lifestyle management, operating from a call centre in Tyneside. Since it was such an unrelated business, Alf and Mark really did not know what to make of it.

The UK complementary business in events management lost interest fairly quickly, largely because of the profile of ATMA's client base. The US competitor submitted a modest bid with a three-year earn-out and a five-year payout. This was turned down.

The UK competitor was genuinely interested, but there was another deal which ultimately took priority.

The successful buyer was the 'wild card'. Empalert has charitable origins and its clients are a mix of governmental, commercial, charitable and member-based organisations. It saw ATMA as a means to access new markets and products that would enhance its service offering, while recognising significant cultural alignment, with shared strong and positive values around staff and customer service.

A good outcome

At the time the deal suited both parties, the financial outcome was good, and both sets of personal aspirations were achieved. Mark and Alf were pleased to be doing the deal with Empalert, which understood the ATMA concept but had no experience of its own and therefore wanted Alf and Mark to stay and help develop the business.

The acquirer was very clear about the expectations around staff retention, and with both Alf and Mark remaining in the business, the staff remained loyal to the business and stayed. One week after the deal completion, Alf and Mark did a joint presentation with the new owners. The main concern was expressed in a common question, 'Are Alf and Mark still around?' Once the staff were reassured on that point, they were confident and comfortable about the future – good for them and good for Empalert as well.

A bottle of whisky

Alf and Mark completed the deal in a very long day, with legal teams, at the acquirer's Tyneside office. It surprised them both that while there had already been several iterations of the sale and purchase agreement, there was still so much ground to cover, in so much detail. They even tried to improve their own earn-out salary package at the eleventh hour, but unfortunately this fell on deaf ears!

When it was all signed and delivered, the acquirers gave each participant a bottle of their corporate personalised whisky, and in terms of celebration, that was that!

BCMS has the final say

From Alf's point of view, the 18-month earn-out was very satisfactory and, now in retirement, he is able to enjoy more time with his family and young children.

Mark's health put him through turmoil. During the sale and the two-month period of due diligence, he was diagnosed with prostate cancer. Following his biopsy he had sepsis twice, with two spells in hospital and robust treatment concurrent with the BCMS process! After the deal, he had a successful operation and recuperated over Christmas.

Having completed the earn-out, Mark had a personal objective to complete his MBA dissertation, enjoy a greater focus on fitness and give time to some charity initiatives. He was also ready for a change of career and had made the decision to do something completely different.

In a strange twist, Mark explains his current situation: 'I enjoyed the experience and was particularly impressed with the entire process during the sale. I found myself thinking there are aspects of what BCMS does that I would love to be involved in, and I do believe I could contribute more besides. My background and expertise and my own business experience fit the SME M&A marketplace that BCMS serves so well. Systemised process is my forte, and that is the BCMS way.'

BCMS subsequently utilised Mark's ability and experience by offering him an appropriate role in the business. The poacher has turned gamekeeper!

Note: In this chapter, real names have been replaced with pseudonyms at the request of the parties involved. All facts are accurate.

Fact file

The business

ATMA operates in the non-profit sector, providing outsourced professional services, including events management, to membership bodies and trade associations.

At the time of disposal the business employed 20 staff in two locations and had a turnover of £1.3 million.

The reason for sale

The shareholders had operated the business for 11 years with a small select client base and were currently testing a route to market to advance the business to its next growth phase. This would require significant investment to capitalise on the opportunity, in terms of marketing and building operational capacity, to attract and take on additional clients.

The majority shareholder was approaching retirement age and the other was at a life stage where he wanted to have a crack at another career.

There was a joint rationale, therefore, to find a buyer with the finance and resources to move the business on to its next stage and provide a simultaneous exit for both shareholders.

The outcome

BCMS Corporate identified 184 potential acquirers, and 26 NDAs were signed. Four prospects entered into negotiative dialogue, and two bids were received.

The successful offer was close to six times EBIT, with 40% cash on completion and 60% tied to an earn-out based on forecast profits over an 18-month period.

Through effective negotiation and as a result of ensuing developments, these terms were improved significantly, so that 60% was paid on completion and the balance settled after only six months.

Both shareholders stayed with the acquiring business for 18 months, but on a diminishing time commitment.

Kohlswa Gjuteri AB

Global reputation

The Swedish company Kohlswa Gjuteri is one of the oldest businesses to be sold by BCMS. It has been manufacturing iron and steel under various guises since 1548 and is based in the small village of Kohlswa, which has just 2,000 inhabitants and is located some 150 km west of Stockholm.

The company has a reputation for quality and excellence, particularly in substantial marine and offshore oil applications. BP, Exxon, Total and other oil companies use Kohlswa swivels for their oil rig mooring chains. Many ships with world-class certification from Lloyds Register, the American Bureau of Shipping and the Norwegian registration foundation DNV are fitted with large propeller blades from Kohlswa.

The business has a global reputation for manufacturing complicated parts which other foundries have difficulty in emulating. During its history this company has been owned as part of the ABB group and subsequently as part of the Electrolux group, with the company's three senior managers acquiring the majority shareholding in 2002.

The team of three

When talking to Hakan Thoreson you sense a 'hands on' MD who loves the positive history of both the business and its location, an MD full of positive energy for the present, and an MD who is even more passionate about the potential for Kohlswa's future. Hakan is an experienced man in his field, and had worked for another steel foundry for 15 years. He was previously an export sales manager and had worked a lot in sales and marketing. An active traveller, he had built up an impressive list of contacts from international trade fairs, as well as direct client relationships in Germany and Switzerland. He also had a range of good personal contacts in offshore operations and shipbuilding, in Stavanger,

Hamburg and Houston. In a nutshell, Hakan's business experience had generated a lot of contacts and a good reputation.

In 2000 he was offered the role of marketing director at Kohlswa. In 2002 Hakan and two senior colleagues – Conny Andersson (Sales Manager) and Anders Wievegg (Planning Manager) – acquired the shares of the business, and were to become a positively formidable team in the company's future development.

This team of three had already proved their skills in previous years, but with the extra freedom and responsibility of owning and directing the business themselves, they began to see some outstanding development. At the time of their share acquisition, the profit was running at zero. This was changed quickly and dramatically, and within five years they had doubled the turnover. While the three retained 94% of the shareholding, 11 other members of staff were given the opportunity to acquire the remaining shares.

Working to live

The team had not purchased the shares with a view to a future trade sale, as Hakan explained: 'I didn't buy to sell, I bought the shares because I wanted to be an entrepreneur. I wanted a future I could enjoy, a future with interesting work. I wanted both the pleasure and responsibility of running the company, and at the same time the opportunity to take care of the people in the village.'

As part of their creative management approach the team had a strategic off-site meeting every second year in interesting or memorable places. In 2003 Iceland was the venue, and in 2005 it was Barcelona. In 2007 the team met in Rome. Rome is a city full of history, of course, but it is also a place of historic world-changing strategic decisions made by global leaders in different generations. And it was this environment that was to lead to a life-changing decision for the team of three. On the rooftop of the Radisson SAS Hotel overlooking the Colosseum and the Basilica di Santa Maria, and with Vatican City in the distance, Anders began to introduce the notion of either beginning to look for a business partner that could help fund growth or selling the business. Anders was seeking to realise some capital, Conny was beginning to look towards retirement, and Hakan was happy to work with them to achieve their aims.

At the time the three were clear that the business was too weak to achieve maximum value, because of lack of funds. But in that historically strategic city, a strategic decision was made: to work on a plan to sell the business. Before the journey home began, a task list of action points had been agreed. The process was set in motion.

Two crises, two outcomes

Before the Rome decision there had been two significant crises during the growth period. Two years after the team purchased the shares (in 2004), the business ran into a serious liquidity problem. Hakan's years of local business engagement were to pay dividends, as good long-term relationships with the local bank enabled the team to put forward a plan that the bank was happy to fund. The experience also positively cemented the team together and led to an innovative scheme of collecting and subsequently selling scrap, which helped to turn the liquidity situation in a positive direction.

A more serious crisis was to test their strength and resolve even further. In January 2007 there was a bad accident in the smelting shop. The company was two full months without smelting capacity. There were all kinds of inevitable losses in finance and production. Kohlswa lost a particularly important client in Germany, together with a number of smaller clients.

During this time, however, several offshore clients wrote to the company, commending it for its strength and quality. For Kohlswa, it felt as though the industry as a whole was getting behind it. With this encouragement and newly energised resolve,

the company managed to secure a number of new clients, and its reputation grew even stronger.

It was this second crisis and its impact that began to form and frame the decision made shortly afterwards in Rome. Hakan put it this way: 'Even with the positive steps that we had made, the two crises had etched firmly into our minds that to take the business on and grow it further would require more strength in the ownership. Thus the notion was born either to sell or to find a partner.'

In Anders' mind this time was an optimal point in the company's growth. The business was generating good profit, and the order book was full for the coming three years. He was convinced it was the right time, and it transpired that he was right.

'The two crises had etched firmly into our minds either to sell or to find a partner.'

From Rome to research

The decision was made during that weekend on the Radisson rooftop, but it was Hakan who was tasked with the resultant action points. On returning home, he began Internet research to produce a shortlist of the companies that could be suitable to act on their behalf. Ten companies were presented to the team, and three of these were ultimately invited to visit. Hakan had also attended a small seminar at which Lars Berglund from BCMS Scandinavia had been presenting. The potential relational contact, and the positive thinking in his own mind as a result of the seminar, placed BCMS Scandinavia as favourite in his mind. As Hakan recalled, 'Lars gave me confidence both personally and in terms of process and system that no-one would do this better. From the outset we had confidence in Lars as a person, and in the BCMS desk research process, to find us the best choice of buyers.

'From the beginning our ideal was to avoid selling to a pure investment company. The best outcome for us would be to sell to a steel manufacturing company. All three of us agreed that we wanted a partner or owner in the foundry or steel business, an acquirer that would understand the value of what we had grown and then develop it further. We were also very committed to working hard to protect both the workforce and the community in which the business is located.'

In August 2007 the three made their first visit to the BCMS headquarters in the UK. Hakan remembers being extremely impressed with the high level of educated people and the scale of the resources that would soon be put to work on their behalf. In November Hakan and Conny made a second trip.

Hakan put his thoughts in this way: 'I had some ideas of looking at companies in India, knowing that Indian companies often want to buy in. We looked at Brazil, Australia, China and South Africa.'

The BCMS results were substantial and fairly speedy: 281 potential acquirers were identified, with 23 subsequent signed

NDAs. From this there was a shortlist of 10 companies which the team considered 'hot ones'. Three advanced negotiation meetings ultimately took place.

Results were substantial and fairly speedy:
281 potential acquirers were identified, with
23 subsequent signed NDAs.

One of the bidders appeared particularly keen, and in the first instance was the only company selected to visit the foundry. Another competitive bidder from Ontario was planning a visit but was dissuaded by the team.

Hakan says: 'I immediately realised how interested the main bidders from Stockholm were. They were clearly hungry, so because of that we could be tough. It was clear to us that they had the money and had made the decision to buy a foundry. We were confident therefore that we could negotiate a good price.

'Equally we did not want to miss the window of opportunity. Timing for the bidder was critical, and we could see that inviting another competitive company could in theory increase our strength in the bidding process. However, we could see it would lose time when that time was critical to retaining the hungry bidder. In our judgment, that lost time could in turn have lost us the key bidder.'

Thus it was that the Canadian competitor was stalled and the final buyer made the decision to buy on 1 July. Lars Berglund together with Kohlswa's lawyer negotiated the final deal. The team of three was delighted with the final outcome. The sale price achieved was initially 33% higher than the first bid.

Subsequently the team got extra money on the basis of a good first-year result. The final outcome was 43% more than the first bid. The team's non-financial aspirations had been met too. The acquirer was an investment company that owned a foundry group.

The sale price achieved was initially 33% higher than the first bid. The final outcome was 43% more than the first bid.

The journey was tougher than expected

Of course, as in every business sale, normal business has to be maintained and decisions around staff involvement and communication made. In Kohslwa's case, one person in accounts did not want to be part of the process and did not want to cooperate. This in turn created some additional work.

From the outset it was decided to keep the staff well informed, albeit in a very conservative and appropriate manner. The team explained that they were looking to grow the business, and that in turn meant they had to find a partner. They also made clear that no-one could predict what the outcome would be. The response from the staff was positive and created no problems. In Hakan's

view it made things considerably easier not having to work with 'hush hush' procedures or pressures.

Hakan thought the due diligence was unnecessarily hard work. As he put it, 'Eighty per cent of the due diligence was not really necessary. It was mandated, but in reality it was wasted time for both buyer and seller.'

The open communication with staff paid off. All the existing staff stayed, and no problem arose on this issue with the acquirer. As part of the negotiation it was agreed that there would be no changes in management or staff. The team of three was asked to remain in the business for three years.

The biggest surprise was that having looked around the world for potential acquirers, and after 281 potential acquirers had been identified, the company found that its final acquirer was just 150 kilometres away in Stockholm. And yet despite the geographical proximity, the team would never have found the buyer through any searches or contacts of their own. It took the BCMS research process to discover that acquirer.

Having looked around the world, and finding 281 potential acquirers, it took the BCMS research process to find the final acquirer - just 150 kilometres away

A lesson in Swedish culture
Hakan provided an insight into Swedish workplace culture that reflected the post-sale experience: 'Swedes don't celebrate like other people. When the deal was finally concluded, we were in the company conference room and we celebrated in that room together with our lawyer and a glass of champagne.'

Far more memorable for Hakan was his second visit to BCMS in the UK. Hakan's football team, Arsenal, were playing Reading, and he asked if there was any chance of getting tickets. BCMS director Steve Rebbettes bought tickets for Conny and Hakan. For both of them it was one of the most memorable personal experiences in the process!

Personal outcomes that differ

Three years have elapsed since the acquisition took place. All three in the team have stayed with the company full time, although in preparation for retirement Conny is now down to 80%. Hakan offers another insight into Swedish culture: 'Almost all Swedes find it normal to get up at 6am and do 40 hours a week at least. Most of us don't want another style of life: I am only 52 years old and I like working, I don't think of retiring.'

For Hakan the process of change has brought some unexpected personal challenges. From his point of view, his work patterns have been changed more than those of his two colleagues. With new 'corporate' owners, inevitably he has had to attend more internal meetings and produce significantly more management reporting information. Hakan finds this dimension a little boring, preferring as he does to spend more time visiting clients and caring for the staff.

However, there has also been a corresponding positive surprise: the feeling of being independent of the bank, and the feeling of being independent of the company. As Hakan says, 'Financial independence means I don't have to work, I don't have to go to the bank and ask for money.

'Now I work with less external stress and pressure. I also have the ability to stop any time I wish. That's freedom.'

Now the bank is calling me, wanting to invest. That pressure has lifted and it's a very rewarding feeling. Life is less stressful. We've spent a little on the house and decorating, and taken a few holidays. However, I do love to work, and now I work with less external stress and pressure. I also have the ability to stop any time I wish. That's freedom.'

Fact file

The business
Kohlswa Gjuteri AB has been manufacturing in iron and steel since 1548. The business has a global reputation for quality and excellence, particularly in substantial marine and offshore oil applications.

The reason for sale
Following two critical business incidents, the three owners had become increasingly aware that to take the business on and grow it would require more strength in the ownership.

The owners wanted an acquirer that would understand the value of the world-class manufacturing which had been achieved, and bring with them the financial and management capacity to develop the potential further.

The outcome
BCMS Corporate identified 281 potential acquirers, with 23 signed NDAs. A shortlist of 10 was agreed, and three advanced negotiation meetings took place, leading to a final negotiation process with the preferred bidder.

JAMES TAYLOR & SON

My feet hurt!

Peter Schweiger's father fled from Nazi Germany after his brother was murdered in 1934. He was interested in orthopaedics and foot supports, with a passion to make people's feet comfortable. At the time of the British abdication crisis in 1936 he took out a patent for a new type of arch support. His mission in life was to bring comfort to every pair of feet. This comfort came first with his foot supports, and later with his particular type of made-to-measure shoes.

The young Peter, later to become MD of James Taylor & Son, first began working for the family business while he was still at school. At that time the business was operating out of the family home, and he remembers the telephone calls day and night that would exasperate his mother as clients began the conversation with the comment, 'My feet hurt.'

After several years of running the business at home and seeing it grow, Peter's father acquired a lease on a shop in Blandford Street, London W1. The building was old and war-damaged. Peter recalls looking out from the top of the number 13 bus on his way to work and seeing the bomb site close by, where Marks & Spencer would later build its head office. During this period his father bought James Taylor & Son, whose owners wanted to retire.

After two years these premises had become too small, and Peter's father acquired the freehold of a shop at 4 Paddington Street, where the business operates to this day. In order to save money in the move, Peter, then aged 9, was tasked with carrying boxes of lasts, stock and equipment 300 yards from Blandford Street to the new premises in Paddington Street, through Grotto Passage.

James Taylor & Son were bespoke and orthopaedic shoemakers, and that was to shape the future of the business.

The shoe doesn't fit

As Peter approached the end of his school education, the question of his own career was raised. Joining the family business was one obvious possibility, but as he had found his father a rather impatient teacher, he began to explore other options with his careers teacher.

He was advised to go into forestry. Peter was one of 4,000 people applying for 40 jobs with the Forestry Commission, but he succeeded. While waiting for the outcome of his application, he worked for six months in the family shop. He remembers the toughest part was the daily commute, something he grew to enjoy in later years.

In stark contrast to the comfortable indoor London routines, Peter's first job in forestry was two years of piecework in a Hampshire forest. This was relentless physical work, day after day. He then spent two years at the forester training school in North Wales, with 40 subjects on the syllabus. When he obtained his certificate, there were no jobs available except in the midge-riddled North of Scotland. He found a job with the London Borough of Hillingdon as a tractor driver and chainsaw operator while he waited for the forestry officer to retire. At the job interview he was deemed 'too commercial' to be suitable for local authority work, but in fact over the years the council implemented many of his 'commercial' suggestions.

The learning curve

Peter decided to rejoin the family business in 1970. His father had died, and his father's business partner was now running the company. The business was operating with significant losses, and Peter had to learn fast. He chose to master every part of the trade, so that he could have confidence in his later management of staff. At the same time, he was attending evening classes to develop his business knowledge. The partner retired in 1972, and 26–year-old Peter found the full responsibility for running the family business resting on his shoulders.

26-year-old Peter found the full responsibility for
running the family business resting on his shoulders.

At first the impact of responsibility, staffing issues, finance and client pressures led to depression. Somehow in the dark days that followed, a simple truth dawned: enjoy it. If he was to survive this process, he had to choose to enjoy the challenge, embrace the opportunity to find solutions, and enjoy the very real difference his shoes would make to the quality of life of the people who wore them.

Because of his youth, and because his father's partner had left the business unexpectedly, the staff wrongly accused Peter of pushing the partner out and threatened to resign. But Peter now had the confidence and experience to find ways to secure the goodwill of the staff, and he began to move the business into healthy returns. The learning curve continued as his bookkeeper was discovered to be embezzling money from the business. The individual was later sentenced to two years in prison.

Peter also faced an unfair dismissal claim by two part-time receptionists. With help from the Forum of Private Business, which gave good advice, a former receptionist gave a glowing testimonial to Peter's generous and caring attributes as an employer, and the case was dropped.

On another occasion, one of Peter's employed shoemakers asked for a loan. When Peter refused, he threw a hammer. As Peter wryly remarked, 'It missed! And on this occasion I wasn't nailed!'

Moving on
Peter's early baptism of fire at a personal and business level accelerated the growth of his resilience and practical wisdom. One of the things he found difficult was perpetually having to juggle priorities and solve problems. As part of his continuing education Peter went to juggling classes: 'The metaphor of juggling is

helpful because it teaches to you to focus on several things at the same time.'

With a growing ability to focus on several issues at once and to handle multiple demands and priorities, Peter was able to take a tough decision which was to prove critical. His father had secured an NHS contract for orthopaedic shoes, which at the time represented a large percentage of the company's turnover and workload, but it ran on very tight margins. The NHS paid slowly, and when it embarked on further reductions in procurement costs, profits were squeezed still more: the business had to survive on a large overdraft. The decision was taken to stop NHS work. Risky and tough though it was, it proved to be significantly beneficial. Trading improved enormously as the company found the right clients at the right prices and served them. Cash flow was reversed, so that instead of trading with the bank's money, the firm traded on what it made from the customers.

A prince, Ali G and Paul Getty

One of the big unknowns in the shoe business, especially with first fittings, is how well the shoes will work out. It is impossible to predict if there will be one interim fitting or multiple fittings. This in turn means frequent people contact. Peter grew to love this contact with a wide range of interesting people. He also loved the invitations that came to fit wealthy people in their own homes.

One Tuesday morning he received a call from Crown Prince Abdullah of Saudi Arabia requesting a fitting. Convinced it was a hoax, Peter insisted he phone the caller back. To his shock he discovered it was real!

The following day he presented his passport and was issued with a visa. On the Friday of that week he was in the air, on his way to a fitting session. Peter was told that His Highness had a preference for Italian designs. Needing inspiration on a range of ideas and options, he called his friends and contacts in the trade press for articles and pictures of Italian designs. When he read the articles on the plane, it dawned on him that most of the designs were for women and were modelled by beautiful and often scantily clad ladies. He remembers the worry of being detained at immigration with his pictures and magazines! Fortunately, however, it proved not to be a problem.

In the course of fitting 14 pairs of shoes over a long weekend, Peter enjoyed hospitality at the Crown Prince's palace, memorably dining with the Royal Family. The extravagantly embroidered tablecloth used at the meal is one of many images etched in his memory.

On another occasion the actor Sacha Baron-Cohen – then better known as Ali G – requested a visit to be fitted for callipers. It was a very unusual request, but was linked to his role as a wounded First World War soldier who becomes a stationmaster in a period movie called Hugo.

An Evening Standard reporter visited the Paddington Street shop one day and noticed a pair of lasts with Paul Getty's name on them. The reporter was asked not to mention it, but inevitably the entrepreneur's name appeared in the Standard. On his next visit to Getty's hospital suite, Peter was understandably apprehensive about how the conversation would go. His fears were confirmed when Getty remarked how much he disapproved of his name being used in an advertisement – but nonetheless he purchased another pair of shoes!

Future thoughts

Thoughts about retirement and succession were the trigger for Peter to begin considering exit strategies. This is the case for roughly half of BCMS Corporate's clients. As he reached the age of 60, he found himself attracted by a BCMS brochure featuring a retired man sitting on a deckchair by the sea in his suit.

Listening to the BCMS presentation, he let his mind roll forward some years and determined his next step would be to get the company more profitable before making the final and irreversible decision to sell.

As these thoughts surfaced, it became clear to Peter that the really important issues for him were to protect all his staff's jobs and equally to ensure continuing satisfactory service to all his customers.

Thoughts about retirement and succession were the trigger for Peter to begin considering exit strategies.

Since neither his children nor his brother's children had any desire to take on the business, Peter knew his responsibility was to secure the right kind of acquirer. He had acquired other shoemakers himself over the years, paying them only on commission, but had often reflected that while this might be the industry norm it was a poor reward for years, often decades, of hard work. These firms had insisted that their customers be well looked after, and he was determined that this should be the case when he sold the business.

The BCMS proposition offered a much more attractive deal, with a substantially wider database of potential acquirers and a better approach with multiple buyers at the negotiation phase.

Peter achieved his short-term goal of improving profitability but became increasingly aware that with no family succession, to be sure the business would progress and that his staff and customers would get the best possible outcome he would need an acquirer capable of bringing the necessary growth and development.

'Without family succession, he would need an acquirer capable of bringing the necessary growth and development.'

If the shoe fits...

When Peter hit the magic age of 65, his peers were retiring, but he had no desire to retire completely and become a gardener/babysitter. He was increasingly determined to find a suitable successor sooner rather than later. In the intervening period he had approached several accountancy firms, checking their terms and comparing them with the BCMS process. He found most accountants' approach was to work out a price for the firm, in response to which potential buyers would negotiate a lower price. In the end it was a straightforward choice for Peter. BCMS offered the likelihood of a much better and wider choice of potential acquirers, as well as a higher value for the business, based on potential.

Peter later explained what had persuaded him to use BCMS: 'Choice was really important to me. BCMS Corporate offers a range of potential acquirers, which meant I could be quite choosy. Having choice meant I was able to turn down two firms because I didn't like their attitude, work ethic or business approach. It put me in a strong position to be highly selective, making sure the final acquirer represented the right deal for me and the family, and also the right deal for staff and customers.'

'It put me in a strong position to be highly selective, making sure the final acquirer represented the right deal'

It's like growing trees
Peter's early experience with forestry was to prepare him for the process of selling, which from his perspective was slow and steady. As he put it, 'When you're growing trees it takes a long time for them to get big, but they will get there. The process does seem surprisingly slow, but one just has to live long enough.'

Peter had this to say about the BCMS team: 'At the two seminars I attended, BCMS were pretty candid and transparent about how the sale process would work. It appeared to me to be a good formula that would work predictably. I was glad that they gave me two mentors, Clare and Mark. Because of their experience, they had seen it all before, so when I had concerns or questions they were a very reassuring professional presence.'

Open season
As soon as the decision was made to put the firm on the market, Peter told all his staff. This is very unusual in BCMS Corporate's experience. When pressed on his reasons for this level of openness and transparency, Peter responded, 'I chose to tell the staff in a team meeting, for a number of reasons. Firstly, as I was at retiring age, they kept asking what my future plans were, as they were understandably concerned about their own future. Secondly, customers were asking similarly penetrating questions. To both I reiterated the reality that it would take time, and would need patience from all of us.' All the staff were grateful for the level of openness and none left.

Diary of the final moments
Peter has kept a diary since 1981. Adapted extracts from his diary

shed a fascinating light on the human moments that occurred for Peter and his wife Hentschy in the final stages of the sale completion.

Friday August 5th: a bright day. I feel a bit apprehensive and yet flat that today will be the day I sell the firm. At the shop, I spent quite a bit of time trying to transfer the funds from the deposit account to the current account and walked down to Marylebone High Street to buy a cake for the firm from Waitrose.

My auditor Robert Rosenthal came in just as I was taking photos of Neal Salisbury's flashy boots with gold and silver zips and high heels. Robert and I went to the office to sort out all the transactions. We drew out director's redundancy for myself and

Hentschy, my wife. Robert worked out the calculations based on the HMRC formula according to length of service. That is tax-free. We hit an issue with Work In Progress. I had calculated it to be £47,000 but Robert's calculation came to £23,000. I explained to Steve the buyer and he was put out, after all a £20,000 difference is not inconsequential. Steve and I went to chat with Andrew Tobias the solicitor and it looked as if the deal might fail. Steve's confidence in our integrity was shaken. Steve then went to see an independent solicitor, leaving my fellow shareholders with me, wondering what to do. Compromise would imply our WIP was wrong.

It was Steve who came up with a solution. He proposed a retainer of £25,000 be held in the solicitors' client account until the WIP could be verified. Paperwork revisions meant the sale would definitely not complete today. I had hoped the signings would happen at 3pm and we would then go the Landmark Hotel for tea. Just after 6, having agreed the share signings would be completed on the following Tuesday, the celebration planned for tea at the hotel went ahead, somewhat later than planned and in a muted and incomplete style.

Tuesday 9th August. Andrew Tobias and I collected two copies of the sale purchase agreement to read before signing. It was written in legal nonsense, so was unintelligible. I asked some questions about how the stock was represented, then decided there was no point in rocking the boat at the last minute! Hentschy arrived and at about 3pm she and I went over to sign the papers. Immediately afterwards Steve wanted to talk to the staff. Hentschy and I took a taxi to Marylebone Station and caught a rather crowded two-car train at 15.57.

Hentschy and I finished the day with a meal together at the Swan in Old Amersham with an upstairs table in a bay window looking out over the high street. We had a glass of sparkling wine.

I was glad the sale had gone through and yet finished the day thinking it is back to business as usual now.

The first of the new lasts

For the final acquirer, Precision 3D Limited, concluding the deal was an important step forward. Precision 3D specialises in software, in particular 3D scanning, enabling new lasts to be made more accurately than by traditional methods, and in a faction of the time. This holds great promise for the future of the business, its staff and the customers. Once the use of this software and scanning equipment has been demonstrated successfully in the London shop, the intention is to replicate the Paddington Street solution at other sites.

The future is here

The outcome has been ideal for Peter. He has no desire to retire, and continues by choice to work four days a week as Managing Consultant. He got a good sale price and remains the landlord, with his brother, leasing the building to the newly owned business. The agreement also promised him a percentage on the turnover for three years post-sale. As he put it, 'I am very motivated to make the business grow and succeed.'

Having an extra day each week for family and friends has been a real pleasure. Peter now has time to engage in philanthropic pursuits with the Rotary Club of St Marylebone and in other ways. Active in the Royal Forestry Society, he has recently planted trees in London to commemorate the great-granddaughters of James Taylor.

He is financially secure, all the staff have been able to stay in employment, the customers have the benefit of an even better service, and the business has great future potential under new ownership with new technology.

Peter still loves coming in to work every day. He still loves the engagement with clients and the outcome of feet feeling comfortable in his shoes. He wants to continue playing his part in foot comfort, and doesn't see that changing any time soon.

Fact file

The business
James Taylor & Son was a family-owned business specialising in handmade footwear and orthopaedic shoes. Based in Paddington Street, London, the business has a reputation for excellence and comfort in footwear.

The reason for sale
Peter Schweiger, the outgoing MD and major shareholder, had reached retirement age and wanted to secure a great future for staff and clients alike. He was also very aware that in order to realise the company's potential, a fresh injection of resource and focus was necessary.

Peter's stated aim was to secure the future for his staff and all his clients. His preference was to continue working as long as possible.

The outcome
BCMS Corporate identified 181 potential acquirers. Twenty-one firms signed an NDA and five entered the final stages of the bidding process. Peter had a clear idea of the kind of acquirer he wanted for the business and was able to turn down two potential acquirers because of work ethic and business attitudes.

The successful bidder was Precision 3D. The deal included a cash sum, and importantly for Peter it has allowed him to remain as Managing Consultant to the business, working four days per week, with commission agreed for the first three years' post-sale turnover. All the staff have continued to work for the acquiring company.

The new owner has introduced great potential for development and growth, in particular with new scanning technology. A 3D scanner now enables more accurate lasts to be made in a fraction of the time required by traditional methods, and the future potential for the firm to grow with new technology is greatly enhanced.

Note: In case you are interested in a custom-made shoe, prices for the first last and first pair of shoes start at well under £2,000, with significant reductions on subsequent shoes. Contact Peter at James Taylor & Son.

HALYARD

A dream and small beginnings

As far back as he can remember, James Grazebrook had wanted to start and run his own business. After working in the Middle East from 1976 to 1979 and saving a proportion of his income, he began to look for the appropriate opportunity to take that first step.

During his search James was given the chance to promote a structure-borne noise reduction device for marine engines, originally developed by GKN and known as the Aquadrive. In a one-room building in Brentwood, Essex, James's new future began.

From the beginning, James had the unusual experience of having two chartered accountants as non-executive directors. This meant that from day one, great systems and great discipline were embedded in the fledgling business, something that would stand the firm in good stead during the future years of growth. As James put it, 'With two accountants on the team, I was never allowed to be without a positive cash flow, a business plan and an acute consciousness of financial control. Two accountants were simply never going to let that happen!'

Rate hike

In 1984, newly married and looking to relocate, James moved the company's operations to Salisbury. The business was already growing, and additional staff were being recruited. At the same time, the decision was made to buy some commercial premises and lease them back to the business. In 1989 the bank base rate went to 15%, making it impossible for the company to afford enough rent to cover the mortgage repayments. After thinking the implications of this through, and with a great deal of goodwill all round, James offered to buy out the other shareholders, and they agreed.

This in turn freed James to take some decisions around product development and business direction. The company had already diversified from its original structure-borne noise reduction device into airborne noise insulation. As a natural development, exhaust systems were now added to the portfolio.

Looking for the right partner in exhaust systems, James travelled to the USA, returning with sales rights for a range of marine silencers manufactured by a US company. This initially proved a great decision: Halyard sold £0.5 million worth in 12 months. Unfortunately, however, things went badly wrong in the US recession in 1991, and the future of the manufacturer was seriously threatened.

As a result, Halyard began to do its own manufacturing in Britain; overnight, the business went from distribution to manufacture. James says, 'We had absolutely no experience and we made some enormous mistakes. At first, our ignorance was a great ally. We had two major boat builders, Fairline and Princess, who both wanted to use the products. Both companies gave us enormous support, actually helping us get where we needed to be.'

Reluctant wives and red tape
In a serendipitous way, reluctant wives and bureaucratic government were both to have a significant influence on Halyard's development. Boat builders were beginning to understand that if they were to succeed in selling a boat, it would commonly be important for the purchaser's wife or partner to support the decision. And for that to happen, 'she' needed to see damp cured, smells eradicated, better navigation equipment, and above all less noise! In essence, major boatbuilders had identified noise reduction as a critical factor in getting wives to support the buying decision.

At around the same time, the German government announced it was going to enforce noise levels on boats using the Bodensee, paving the way for the EU to enforce noise reduction legislation throughout its territory. Trade federations across Europe approached Halyard, offering to help arrange significant EU financial support if James and the team could help them to work out how the continent's boat industry could achieve the newly reduced levels.

James determined not to accept the grant, arranging instead for the trade federations to manage the money for the public good. That way, as James said, 'We could preserve both our independence and our integrity.' By the time the regulations were enforced in 2006, virtually every boatbuilder could comply. As a result of its part in the process, Halyard had developed and protected significant intellectual property. Every presentation of the new compliance products had Halyard's name embedded in it, and James would often be asked to deliver the technical content for those presentations. The process stimulated extensive changes in marine exhaust silencing, as a result of which Halyard won a Queen's Award for Innovation in 2006. Unsurprisingly, exhaust sales increased dramatically, from £0.5 million out of £1.5 million turnover in the 1990s to £5 million out of £6 million turnover at the time of acquisition.

A further innovative thought, which occurred at the start of the project, was to find a university that specialised in this unique field and endeavour to get them involved. Thus it was that a great relationship developed between the Halyard team and the Institute of Sound and Vibration Research at Southampton University. The university's academic input added an intellectual rigour over the years that followed, and while working in this partnership Halyard won a second Queen's Award for Innovation.

Innovation and growth

With two Queen's Awards, the formal academic support, and the technical drive from Design Director Graham Clapp, the Halyard team found courage to consider much bigger applications, with substantially increased horsepower. In those early days the thought of a 500-hp engine would be fine, but the idea of a 1,000-hp application would cause significant anxiety! Today

applications of up to 4,000 hp are well within the comfort zone. Records of all sorts began to be broken: the top-end system in 2000 was a £50,000 exhaust on a 50-metre sailing boat, surpassed in 2008 by £200,000 for an exhaust system for an 86-metre motor yacht.

As the size of boats increased, other factors became evident. It cost the same to sell an exhaust system for a 200-hp application as it did to sell one for a 2,000-hp application. Two subcontractors were supplying the stainless steel elements and exhaust hoses respectively. Acquiring these two subcontractors enabled Halyard to benefit from the profits these firms had been making from their supply. In turn this facilitated substantial growth. Halyard doubled its turnover twice over, and grew from 30 staff to 80 over a five-year period.

Early thoughts of selling

In 2001 James was approached by an intermediary who wanted to introduce someone potentially interested in acquisition. With hefty school fees at the time, James found himself initially attracted by the proposition. However, the potential buyer was going to borrow heavily to achieve the purchase. That, coupled with the fact that he didn't particularly warm to the individual, led James to pull out of the deal.

In 2006 a bright young sales director joined the Halyard team. He had earned a good reputation in the marine industry and inspired the management team to consider an MBO. The plan was for James to stay on the board and have an interest in the company's future. Involving a private equity firm in the process, they discovered the systems and processes of their then finance director were not up to the standard that the private equity firm required. At the same time, a move of premises had produced a short-term profitability issue. For the second time James found himself troubled by the levels of potential debt involved, in this case for his own team, if they proceeded with the MBO option. They decided to put the MBO on the back burner.

However, the potential buyer was going to borrow heavily to achieve the purchase. That, coupled with the fact that he didn't particularly warm to the individual, led James to pull out of the deal.

James said later: 'An MBO inevitably causes the management team to take their eye off the ball. In an MBO the unique factor is that the vendor is working with the buyers, and their interests potentially oppose each other. That creates a tension that doesn't exist in a normal sale. It can be divisive, especially if the management is buying from the founder.

'The work involved in the MBO for the team and the workload imposed by a private equity house is way above what's required for bank funding. This all got me thinking that I needed to go and find another route.'

> *'An MBO inevitably causes the management team to take their eye off the ball. That creates a tension that doesn't exist in a normal sale. I chose a lawyer from BCMS's panel and they really did live up to their promises.'*

Preparing for the sale

Recessionary pressures in 2008 forced many boat manufacturers to make deep cuts. Coming to the conclusion that he didn't want to be running the business in 10 years' time, James had been encouraged by his several advisers to consider planning for a sale.

James found himself following parallel lines of thought, both converging ultimately on a successful sale. To face whatever bad debt or other challenges the recession might throw at the business, James resolved to maintain the bank balance above £300,000. At the same time, the team worked hard to get margins up and overheads down, achieving a profit increase of 2.5% between 2008 and 2011. For James the outcome was doubly positive: as he began to take firm steps to exit, the business became an even more saleable proposition.

The right partner....

James reflected on his choice of disposal partner: 'When it came to the important question of who should sell my business, the first thought was to consider an accounting firm. What we soon discovered was that accountancy firms are understandably ~ountants first and M&A firms second. They can rifle-shot a ᶠor a large company with one or two prospective buyers with ᵉntiality and accuracy. What they cannot do is achieve the volumes of potential buyers that BCMS can. We wanted to maintain confidentiality, but we really did want someone to approach 200 to 300 potential buyers and give us choice. What we really wanted in an ideal world was 10 really interested buyers and four or five good offers.'

Having seen dozens of BCMS Corporate brochures over the years, James decided to visit the company's Kingsclere office. He determined to arrive early as part of his assessment of the staff and the environment. While waiting in reception, he found himself surrounded by details of hundreds of successful deal completions. Working his way with some interest through these, he saw two firms that he knew well.

Subsequently James contacted one of these owners, who spoke very highly of the BCMS process and impressed on James the importance of choosing the proposed deal leader as an individual, not just BCMS as a company. James later described it like this: 'We chose BCMS as the best provider for a likely sale of our business for maximum value. We also chose our deal leader, Ian, who was a reassuring constant from the day it started to the final lunch together after completion.'

Reasons for sale
Several factors in James's mind contributed to his final decision to sell the business. Aware that regulations coming into effect in 2016 would limit the amount of nitrous oxide used in the technical processes, he found himself thinking, 'The business should invest in this technology; James Grazebrook shouldn't.' This insight clarified his own thinking: the company had reached a size where something more than his skill set was necessary to take it forward. James was clear he wanted the best possible future for all his staff, and he wanted the best possible future outcome for the Halyard brand.

James also had personal aspirations to fulfil. He began to imagine a future with a good pension pot, far fewer telephone calls, and an empty email inbox.

*The company had reached a size
where something more than his skill
set was necessary to take it forward.*

As a keen supporter of apprenticeship and training programmes, he has always enjoyed working with young people and watching them develop. James wanted to spend more time doing this, potentially with disadvantaged young people, as well as working with the Royal National Lifeboat Institution (RNLI) and doing charitable work for the Worshipful Company of Shipwrights. It was important to him to have more time available for these activities, as well as for other more personal pursuits: long-distance walking, deer stalking and working on a 12-acre project at home.

It was also the right time for the family. During the last two years James had been both CEO and Sales Director, a highly demanding time for him and for his hugely supportive family. He would often emerge from his study at home at 8pm, have a snack, and then go back for another two to three hours. The process was unrelenting, and at some point, for everyone's sake, a change had to be made.

The BCMS process close up
Confidentiality was naturally and appropriately preserved throughout the acquisition process. Three co-directors, all of them option shareholders, were on board from the outset, but no-one else knew until the day after the sale.

James reflected later on the process: 'The BCMS deal leader and team were first class, and BCMS helped us to understand early on that we needed to work out the reasons for the buyers' interest in the business. no-one was interested in why we wanted to sell! BCMS gave me a lot of coaching and help in the way I presented the business and spoke to potential buyers.

'We have always had extremely high standards of management information. In particular, our systems were a help in producing the forward-looking or "synergy" business plan, so essential in helping potential buyers understand what the business could be worth in their hands, which is critical to achieving serious offers.'

The outcome
After 221 potential acquirers had been identified and 51 NDAs signed, a number of interested companies started structuring their bids, and six made formal offers. James chose to disqualify a couple of potential bidders because of their high borrowing. He

did not want the future of the business to be blighted or hamstrung by high levels of debt.

The buyer chosen by James genuinely had available cash, which meant zero borrowing – a factor which in the light of previous experiences James found enormously attractive. He trusted the buyer too, and as he put it, 'Believing what someone is saying makes life easier.'

For James, the involvement of his wife was critical. Although she was involved on the sidelines 'in principle and not in detail', James found her support as a sounding board invaluable. A common challenge for sellers is the reality that confidentiality makes it impossible to share at any depth with anyone else. Her people judgment skills were also invaluable as she met a number of potential buyers and helped James in his choices. Halyard's able finance director also worked very closely with James throughout the process – a trusted source of accurate information as well as impartial advice.

While James was delighted to find the right buyer, it was also crucial to negotiate an appropriate final deal, not least in terms of job security for his loyal staff. Many of them had been serving loyally for more than 20 years and had been central to the continued growth and success of the business. For a number of them, particularly those at factory level, their experience with Halyard had been life-changing. James was concerned to structure a sale which gave them all a sound future.

The lawyers' surprise

It's not often that lawyers' surprises are pleasant ones. This story is one exception. At a meeting in a high-rise building in Milton Keynes, both sets of solicitors had done their preparation work: all they had to do was exchange papers. As James remarked, 'They really did live up to their promises. Every single piece of paper had been dealt with the night before, so the actual completion meeting took only 40 minutes. Once heads of agreement are signed, the choice of lawyer is as important as choosing BCMS in the first place. I met three lawyers, two at the suggestion of BCMS and one I already knew. I chose one of BCMS's panel and I have never regretted that choice.'

'They really did live up to their promises. Every single piece of paper had been dealt with the night before, so the actual completion meeting took only 40 minutes... I met three lawyers, two at the suggestion of BCMS and one I already knew. I chose one of BCMS's panel and I have never regretted that choice.'

These boots were made for walking

James remains very positive about the deal, and also about his own ongoing role in the business. He has agreed to stay on part time as a director and continues for now to manage three major accounts. Handing over some of the functions he has enjoyed for years has been a small challenge, as has been the fact that the new team is better at handling some of the tasks!

With more time available now and even more in the future, James has been able to do more walking and become more immersed in everything else he plans to pursue with regard to apprentices, young people and the RNLI.

And finally, a happy postscript to this story is that four months after the sale of Halyard, the New Year's Honours included an OBE for James for his services to the marine industry.

Fact file

The business
Halyard is the European leader in the design and manufacture of marine exhaust systems, with a profound understanding of controlling exhaust noise in boats up to 92 metres in length. The company's mission is the 'science of silence' and it offers a range of products fulfilling this promise, centred on exhaust-silencing systems.

The reason for sale
After owning and running the business for 30 years, James Grazebrook wanted to be free to pursue some philanthropic and leisure activities. He was also aware that a new skill set was necessary to take Halyard to the next level of achievement.

James wanted to secure the future for all his staff and also wanted to ensure that the Halyard brand could grow to its full potential.

The outcome
BCMS Corporate identified 221 potential acquirers; 51 signed an NDA and 11 companies entered into negotiative dialogue, with six making formal offers. The final offer accepted was from a private investor, with a cash sum on completion and a further sum linked to future growth.

All the staff have been retained, and with the new owner the business is set to grow. James continues to work with the business in a part-time capacity and now has time to pursue philanthropic and leisure activities.

MPC DATA

A mistake made good at the Royal Oak

Mike Coombs and Steve Harper had been working together in the early 1980s for Cifer, a company that specialised in customised computer terminals. The company was hot on innovation and had grand plans to develop its desktop computers, but made a fatal mistake by deciding not to pursue IBM compatibility. The rest, you could say, 'is history'.

Inevitably changes began to happen at Cifer, and Mike left to begin a business of his own. A few months later Steve was offered some consultancy work by another ex-colleague, and over a pint at the Royal Oak pub one evening, he and Mike decided to combine forces. Steve duly took a 50% share of the newly formed MPC Data Ltd.

At Steve's leaving party, Cifer employee Alan Rowe said to Mike and Steve, 'I'll join you,' and subsequently became the third shareholder-director. At Alan's leaving party, Simon Pooley made the same move.

In the early months these four were the team, and for a year they worked from home. The business grew quickly, and it became necessary to find somewhere to house the team and to enable growth. Their first office was a rental in Trowbridge above the local pizza shop, where the extra space enabled them to headhunt more employees from Cifer. It also meant the team could begin recruiting students. Before long the office was bursting at the seams.

Lessons in business development

In those early years both Mike and Steve had substantial long-term contracts that they had brought into the business. All four in the initial team had their heads down, fulfilling this contract work. However, when both sources of contract work dried up, they found themselves with four mouths to feed and virtually no work to sustain them or the business.

The issue needed a strategic solution if they were to grow into something more than just a cooperative team of consultants. Alan therefore took on the role of finding new business, with Steve responsible for contract work to fund the business in the meantime.

As Steve put it, 'When we started I was 29 years of age and uninitiated in the need for a sales and marketing system that would keep the business growing. However, the steep learning curve meant we got ourselves onto an even keel rather quickly as we learned about the need to devote ourselves to sales and marketing. The reality was we were all qualified electrical and software engineers, and none of us realised just how important systemised sales and marketing was.'

In fact it was to be less daunting than the team originally feared. Their work was always technically challenging and often at the cutting edge of technology. At the time, few people possessed the requisite skills, and the absence of offshore supply then meant there was little price pressure. MPC soon discovered it was able to sell well on its technical capability and engineering excellence.

Alan's sales work began to pay off: a successful sales funnel was built with household names that in time became long-term customers. These included Teradyne, Sony Broadcast and Hitachi Microsystems (now Renesas), a client still with the business today.

Great memories and early growth
At this early stage Steve was heavily involved in technical work, typically with tight deadlines with no leeway on delivery. Projects were varied, innovative and technologically satisfying – from developing high-availability, high-bandwidth networking equipment to working on the first RDS radio transmission systems; from fish-farm harvesting systems to baby heart monitors; from telephony line testing systems to early retail kiosk

and point of sale systems.

Steve remembers one early project, developing the software for a tomato-harvesting machine. The technology MPC developed could recognise the colour of tomatoes, which enabled the machine to select perfectly ripe tomatoes while rejecting those that were under- or over-ripe. It could also identify stones that happened to be the size and shape of tomatoes. With its leading-edge position and multiple projects of this kind, MPC attracted quality staff.

This early success meant MPC was rapidly outgrowing its premises and again had to look for more space. The old gas warehouse in Bradford on Avon was purchased and renovated. With this new location, a great working environment and interesting work, MPC continued to find excellent staff. MPC's reputation and the quality and breadth of its competence also created strong demand for its services. The team soon grew to 12 employees, while continuing to attract more customers and secure larger projects.

Microsoft's vision a new dawn for MPC

Part of the process of growth involved Microsoft. Bill Gates had a 'Windows everywhere' vision for Microsoft, with plans for a version of its operating system which would work on smaller-scale devices such as vending machines, printers, photocopiers and even watches. In a move that would play a significant role in MPC Data's future, Microsoft turned to a local Seattle-based company called Bsquare to develop the 'Compact' version of Windows.

Microsoft knew that makers of traditional electronics-based devices such as vending machines, photocopiers etc would need a great deal of expert assistance to produce equipment based on 'Windows CE', as it became known. It therefore established a worldwide network of systems integrators with the skills to support customers when they took these products to market. In the mid-1990s, MPC became one of only two UK companies accredited to the Microsoft programme.

New century, new thinking
The factors that had contributed to growth in the 1980s and 1990s were inevitably changing, and so too were the aspirations of the key players. Mike Coombs wanted to retire, and in preparation for this, existing employees Simon Pooley and Phil Buckley were appointed as directors. Mike began to transition out of the business.

Both Phil and Steve see this as a critical turning point, the point at which significant changes began. Steve remembers thinking, 'We are all a similar age and have been able to buy Mike out, but that option is unlikely to be available to us in the future. We need to begin thinking about a different kind of exit plan.'

> *'We need to begin thinking about a different kind of exit plan.'*

The rise of low-cost off-shore supply made the market more competitive, and MPC started coming under greater price pressure. The business was nevertheless growing; Alan and Phil took greater responsibility for business development, while Steve assumed the role of MD, with responsibility for finance and a less hands-on role. For Steve, some of the joy was evaporating out of his work: it was becoming more of a job and less fun, and he knew he didn't want to be trapped in it for ever. The team realised that they could not carry on like this for long, and Steve and Alan began to be concerned that when the time came for them to exit the business, there might not be anyone with the right resources to take it on.

In 2005 the business moved to a purpose-built location in Trowbridge with 8,000 square feet of space, and they had plenty of vision to fill that space with growth. At the same time the team agreed a partial MBO, which gave Phil and Simon a stake in the

business. That year also saw the introduction of two new board members, for the first time from outside the business: Frank Breeze, who brought wide experience of sales and marketing, and Kevin Heawood, who was well known and respected throughout the industry. Kevin had previously led another UK software company through its sale to a US acquirer and was to bring a wide range of business development and commercial experience that was vital to the development of MPC Data, while Frank went on to lead MPC Data's US subsidiary until the acquisition.

Despite the increasing competition, the MPC management team believed there was a lot of future opportunity and embarked on executing a five-year plan, with the intention that Phil would lead a genuine full MBO by 2010/2011. The proliferation of low-cost development centres around the world made differentiation essential, so MPC began to focus on business areas where customers would pay a premium for a unique level of technological expertise together with the company's well-earned reputation for superlative quality. But the plan was about to be shaken by two unexpected storms.

MPC began to focus on business areas where customers would pay a premium ....but that plan was about to be shaken by two unexpected storms.

Not quite as planned!

In 2007 a downturn began that would take its toll on MPC. R&D is often an early casualty at such times, and this was to hit the newly moved business hard. In 2008 the directors took a 25% pay cut, and for the first time in MPC's history redundancies were announced, with seven staff losing their jobs. These were tough times for the business, and they took the wind out of the sails of the planned MBO. With the state of the market, the risk attached to a leveraged buyout was too much for Phil or any of his colleagues to contemplate. Any plans would have to wait for the upturn. And worse was about to come.

In January 2009, Steve developed a serious heart condition. While not immediately life-threatening, it was debilitating. In mid-2009 Phil was also diagnosed with a serious illness. This second health issue immediately turned the future plans upside down: everything was now unknown. Phil was away from work for eight months, and the question in his mind was would he even want to come back and work – and if he did, would he still be keen on the planned exit?

These two illnesses were significant contributing factors in the team's thinking and planning towards the possibility of a different future for the business. Attending a BCMS seminar in Exeter, Steve found the message from the presenters struck a chord, clarifying his thinking about securing a future for everyone in the business while providing options for both him and Phil if they should need to exit quickly.

Determined that MPC should have a secure future that was not dependent on the MBO option, the team engaged BCMS, and the process of a business sale started in early 2010.

The right time

Meanwhile, the business had recovered somewhat from the downturn. Microsoft had affirmed that there was a greater need for its skill set in the USA, so a new office was opened in Washington state, enabling growing partnerships with US companies. Phil's temporary absence and Steve's own health scare had necessitated bringing in an extra layer of management, a reorganisation that ultimately had positive outcomes in the business.

For Steve the time was right. It was rare for him to feel personally fulfilled in the business now, his own health and Phil's health brought additional worries which spilled over into concern for his own long-term well-being. The technology that he loved rarely played any part in his life, and he felt he didn't have the energy he needed to run the business and keep up to date with technology change.

Added to this was the challenge of employing 50 staff, many of whom had been with the business for more than 20 years. These staff wanted and deserved new technical challenges, and many of them were ready for an environment that could expand their career advancement. It was in everyone's interests for a new home to be found.

Finding the right home

Steve and Phil were determined to find the right home for the business, staff and clients alike. The whole MPC team were impressed with the BCMS team at the initial business evaluation consultation.

Steve recalled, 'We used to talk to our accountants – who were good accountants – about selling the business, and they were always keen to engage with us. But I felt it would be like putting up a 'For Sale' sign. What impressed us was the BCMS process – the fact that BCMS was proactive in finding multiple potential acquirers of the right kind gave us the feeling we were more in control of the sale process.'

'We'd had two approaches in the past which were not a good fit for our staff or us. With BCMS's proactivity we were going out there, not waiting for an acquirer to pick us off a shelf. We met a lot of companies that we simply would not have met in any other way. This in turn gave us a choice, and that choice was critical to us.'

'In our view, a number of potential acquirers didn't really understand what we did. Two wanted part of the business but not all of it, and again we never really felt that they "got what we did" and we thought they were definitely not the right home for us.'

'We used to talk to our accountants about selling the business, and they were always keen to engage with us. But I felt it would be like putting up a 'For Sale' sign.'

'Ultimately there was only one company that really felt like home for us and our team, and that was the final acquirer, Bsquare. Bsquare got what we did, having been involved in the same technology since the outset. Their lack of European presence without MPC meant that the acquisition was a great fit for their long-term strategy too. For us, our people are the only true asset; from my first meeting with Bsquare's CEO I knew the same was true of them. This was the right home.'

Keeping it quiet

From the outset of the sale process, it was agreed that it would be Steve's responsibility to deal with BCMS, while others stepped up to take on some of his workload.

During 2010, Phil's improving health enabled him to rejoin the business as Deputy Managing Director. Phil fully engaged with Steve in the business sale process; they worked together in the prospective acquirers meetings and shared the load of both running the business and satisfying the inevitable demands for detailed information that came from the eventual acquirer and their team.

'As a technology company,' Steve recalled, 'we were paranoid that someone would find out what was happening. But the way that BCMS dealt with confidentiality was excellent. It never once leaked out, despite all our worries. No staff members knew until we told them on the day the deal went through, when we could give them the complete picture.'

'We were paranoid that someone would find out what was happening. No staff members knew until we told them on the day the deal went through.'

Having the right lawyer

Steve and Phil observed that having the right lawyer for MPC was critical to the successful outcome: 'BCMS introduced us to Mark Hodge of Stuart Hodge, and they were just brilliant. Our acquirer was Nasdaq-listed and had a very capable team of experienced lawyers; having Stuart Hodge on our side was outstanding, and their team worked tirelessly.' The acquirer's team was sent from the USA for the final fortnight of the legal process. Right up to the day of the final signing there was no certainty it would happen. Even on the last day, a Sunday, the acquirer's CFO was assiduous in protecting their interests.

'Our acquirer was Nasdaq-listed and had a very capable team of experienced lawyers; having BCMS-recommended lawyers Stuart Hodge on our side was outstanding'

For both Phil and Steve, having a deal facilitator and a deal leader was very powerful in meetings with all the potential acquirers. 'If there was anything difficult to say, the deal leader was there to say those things, and also there to stop us saying what we shouldn't. It was very positive and very powerful: it made us feel that we were in control of the process, even at the times when it wasn't completely plain sailing.'

The new home – good for the whole family

Twelve months previously, the MPC team had set out to find a good home for the business as a whole and for the staff in particular. The acquirer Bsquare fitted this bill well. US stock exchange rules meant the staff could not be told of the acquisition for 12 hours. Phil and Steve gathered everyone together and explained the journey of the past 12 months and the acquisition itself. BSquare's CEO (who had come over to finalise the deal) then talked about the future and his exciting vision for their new acquisition. Because BSquare valued their people in the same way as MPC Data did, Steve and Phil were able to negotiate good share options for MPC Data staff. Future success would now be personally rewarding for all concerned, and unsurprisingly all the staff have stayed on.

By the time of the acquisition, Phil had made a full recovery from his illness and took over the lead of the UK business, becoming the General Manager of MPC Data Limited – BSquare's newly acquired 'UK Development Centre'. He has led the business on behalf of the US acquirer ever since.

For Steve, the final celebrations took place with the lawyers' team from Stuart Hodge, followed by a small celebration at home with his wife and two children. Already he has been able to spend more time at home with his wife and more time with the children when they are home from university.

Steve now has more time to work on his golf handicap and to take up new activities and interests, especially since a surgical intervention in 2011 which rectified his heart condition. He is also free to re-engage with technology, getting his mind and skills back onto the leading edge, which is where he loves to be. As some of his friends put it, 'You're a lot more chilled than you used to be.'

FOREWORD

B CMS was founded by the Rebbettes family 23 years ago and since then I have been directly involved in our public seminars with well over 20,000 delegates in the UK and 10,000 more in the USA, China and South Africa.

During that time I've been generally comfortable with our sales approach and sales literature, but there's been a persistent niggle, increasing in recent months, that I've been unable to shake off.

It felt as if we were missing something important, something not directly sales-related, but something really important in the minds of owners and shareholders considering the possibility of selling a business.

Any professional sales process will focus on the benefits being offered. BCMS of course does that, and I hope we do it well. But what I really wanted BCMS to address was the human interest factor. What is it really like to sell a business? What are the stresses and strains? What does it feel like after it's all over and the reality sinks in?

What's the process of disposal like? How tough are the negotiations? How do you choose a lawyer? How important and how easy is it to keep the sale confidential? What does it truly feel like in the lawyer's office when the final signature is applied and, with the ink still wet, the funds are transferred?

This book is intended to answer these questions and much more. I do hope you enjoy these stories and find them intriguing, interesting and maybe in parts a little moving. Above all, I hope it answers some of the questions that are in your mind as you consider what for many of us is the most significant commercial decision of our lives: shall I sell my business?

David Rebbettes, Founding Director and Commissioning Editor

Fact file

The business

MPC Data Ltd is a well-known and respected name with a 25-year track record of success in the embedded software market. The company is recognised as operating at the leading edge of technology developments in the industry.

The reason for sale

Having bought out their partner, Steve Harper and Alan Rowe brought Phil Buckley and Simon Pooley onto the board of MPC Data. This new team planned to work towards an MBO to be led by Phil, over the following five years. However, the downturn in the economy and serious health concerns at the time for two of the team left Phil and Steve looking for a home for the business – the right home for both staff and clients.

The outcome

BCMS Corporate identified 321 potential acquirers, and 41 NDAs were signed. Seven negotiative dialogues were conducted and two final offers considered, with a final deal value of approximately £3.75 million.

The acquirer was Bsquare, an American firm with great growth potential and a good grasp of the unique value MPC and in particular its staff could add to the combined operation. Bsquare has proved to be the right home for MPC Data, the company's staff have been granted share options, and its clients now have access to a worldwide organisation with an even broader skill set.

The outcome has enabled the four main shareholders to achieve their aspirations, both personal and financial.

Phil has gone on to become General Manager of MPC Data.

ABOUT BCMS CORPORATE

B CMS Corporate was established in 1989. Its mission – to become established as the UK market leader for selling privately owned companies for maximum value. Today, BCMS Corporate employs over 240 staff with an international presence spanning Europe, America, Asia and Africa.

Realise your dreams
Our clients choose us because they want to realise their dreams, and what really sets us apart is our ability to create a market of bidders.

We work from the premise that value is determined by the buyer and not necessarily by prevailing market conditions. In other words, we promote the value of your company on the basis of its future potential rather than its past performance. Because we think differently, we are able to achieve significantly higher sales values. It's that outcome that truly enables dreams to be realised.

Why do so many business owners choose us?
As a privately owned business ourselves, we understand that when you are seeking to sell your company, it's personal. The stories in this book will resonate with you because your business too is the product of a lifetime of hard work and commitment.

Business owners choose BCMS for a variety of reasons: solid industry endorsements, hundreds of success stories like the few in this book, and perhaps most of all because BCMS sells companies for such good values.

What BCMS offers is simply this: working ethically on your behalf, we will help you to sell for maximum value.

The leaders in UK business sales
Over the past 20 years we've built up a reputation based on trust, integrity and mutual respect. In fact, we're proud recipients of the coveted Coutts Bank Family Business of the Year Award.

BCMS Corporate also holds and maintains a 'Dun & Bradstreet Rating 1', which indicates the highest level of creditworthiness and minimum risk of failure. This rating has been recognised as a leading predictive indicator for assessing company risk and prospects. Only 15% of all UK companies are in this category.

Other endorsements

BCMS is widely endorsed by banks, financial institutions, lawyers, accountants and trade/professional bodies, including:

• Coutts	• Stuart Hodge
• Kleinwort Benson	• ASB Law
• Brodies	• BPE Law
• Thomas Eggar	• AVN
• Deutsche Bank	• Accountancy age

The next step

If you find the content of this book interesting, maybe even inspiring, there are two easy ways to find out more, and importantly to find out what your business might be worth in the event of a sale, now or in the future.

You can attend one of the many free half-day seminars held across the UK each month entitled 'A refreshingly different approach to selling your business for its maximum value' or you can attend a free business evaluation consultation at your own premises or at one of the BCMS Corporate offices.

For further information please call 01635 296 616 or you can email us at confidential@bcmscorporate.com

Please note: all enquiries are treated in strictest confidence, and any communication will only take place with your designated contact details and with your agreement.

A BOOK WITH A PHILANTHROPIC AIM

Over the years since founding BCMS in 1989 we have been engaged in a number of philanthropic activities. It's part of our values: genuinely wanting to give back, and to make a difference to the poor and disadvantaged.

One of our charitable endeavours is the BCMS Poor and Needy Benefit Trust. This funds a school in India, providing an education for 370 children from poor homes at any one time, and has recently been extended to incorporate permanent accommodation for 50 orphans and 25 widows.

BCMS director Steve Rebbettes says, 'We regard it as a real privilege to be able to help the children, the widows, their carers and teachers in India. Visiting India on a regular basis reminds us how fortunate we are and makes us redouble our efforts to do more charitable work both in India and at home.'

Every copy of I Sold Up distributed will result in a donation of £1 to this worthwhile cause. We estimate that this will exceed £5,000 annually. Details will be published from time to time on the BCMS Corporate website.

For current information and recent stories on the work of this fund, please visit www.bcmscorporate.com